LOCOMOTION PAPERS

The Mangotsfield to Bath Line

including the story of Green Park Station

by
Colin G. Maggs

THE OAKWOOD PRESS

© Oakwood Press & Colin G. Maggs 2005

First published 1992
Second Edition 2005

British Library Cataloguing in Publication Data
A Record for this book is available from the British Library
ISBN 0 85361 634 5

Typeset by Oakwood Graphics.
Repro by Ford Graphics, Ringwood, Hants.
Printed by Cambrian Printers, Aberystwyth, Ceredigion.

Warmley view up *c.*1960. The down signal has two arms, the upper of which would not have been obscured by the road bridge. The clock situated on the wall, left, between the two pairs of windows was two-faced, the other face being in the waiting room.

Lens of Sutton

Title page: BR Standard class '5' 4-6-0 No. 73015 at Green Park with a train to Temple Meads, and BR Standard class '4' 2-6-4T No. 80147 (*left*) with a train to Bournemouth *c.*1965.   *Dr T.R.N. Edwards*

Front cover: Ex-S&DJR class '7F' 2-8-0 No. 53810 with an up goods, 16th July, 1963, below Kelston Park getting up speed to tackle Bitton bank.   *Author*
Rear cover, top: Class '8F' 2-8-0 No. 48309 on 4th April, 1965. The former Midland Railway shed is on the right, while above the roof of the breakdown train, left, is the roof of the ex-S&DJR shed.   *Author*
Rear cover, bottom: Diesel-hydraulic No. D1028 *Western Hussar* at Bath Green Park with the 12.25 pm to Bristol Temple Meads, 23rd October, 1965.   *Author*

Published by The Oakwood Press (Usk), P.O. Box 13, Usk, Mon., NP15 1YS.
E-mail: sales@oakwoodpress.co.uk
Website: www.oakwood-press.co.uk

Contents

Finger boards at Green Park c.1965.   *C. Steane*

Bath (Green Park) train shed on 13th February, 2005.   *Author*

Introduction

Bath, Queen City of the West, has been a place of importance since very early times, tending to specialise in health or the recreational side of life. The Romans eagerly utilised the hot mineral springs to feed their baths, which fell into disuse as the Anglo-Saxons preferred country to town life. Edgar, first King of England, was crowned in Bath Abbey on Whit Sunday 973. Following the doldrums of Medieval and Elizabethan eras as far as Bath was concerned, the population remaining at about 1,000 for 500 years, three very remarkable men co-operated to improve the city.

Richard Nash, commonly called Beau Nash, a gamester who had been in the fastest set at Oxford, came to Bath in 1704 and, elected as Master of Ceremonies, changed society to conform to a strict etiquette. Instead of strolling under trees in the Grove (now Orange Grove) and dancing on the bowling green, visitors now enjoyed music in the Pump Room and handsome Assembly Rooms specially erected for their gatherings.

Ralph Allen, who had already made his fortune as a mail contractor, in his role as a quarry owner was anxious to prove the building value of Bath stone and brought John Wood to the city to construct outstanding classical squares and crescents.

It was the exploitation of this stone which caused a very early railway to be built in 1731. It enabled large blocks weighing upwards of four tons to be carried economically from Combe Down to the River Avon at Widcombe one and a half miles distant and 500 feet below. Loaded wagons descended the gradient of 1 in 10 by gravity, horses being used as motive power on the level and to draw each empty wagon uphill. The timber rails were set at a gauge of 3 ft 9 in. and on them ran the wagons' flanged wheels. Ralph Allen died in 1764 and shortly afterwards his railway was dismantled. The population of Bath in 1750 was about 9,000, in 1801 34,150 and in 1841, the year the Great Western Railway (GWR) was opened from Bristol to London, 53,206.

The spa continued to be used through Victorian times, while a certain amount of industry developed, particularly Stothert & Pitt's, iron founders and crane builders. Because of such easy access to Bath from all parts of the kingdom, particularly following the opening of the Midland Railway's (MR) branch in 1869, the city became an educational centre, with five large boarding schools.

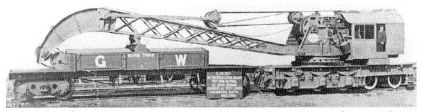

Although Stothert & Pitt mostly manufactured dockside cranes, in 1910 they built this 36 ton breakdown crane for the GWR. It lifted a test load of 45 tons at 20 ft radius.
Author's Collection

5

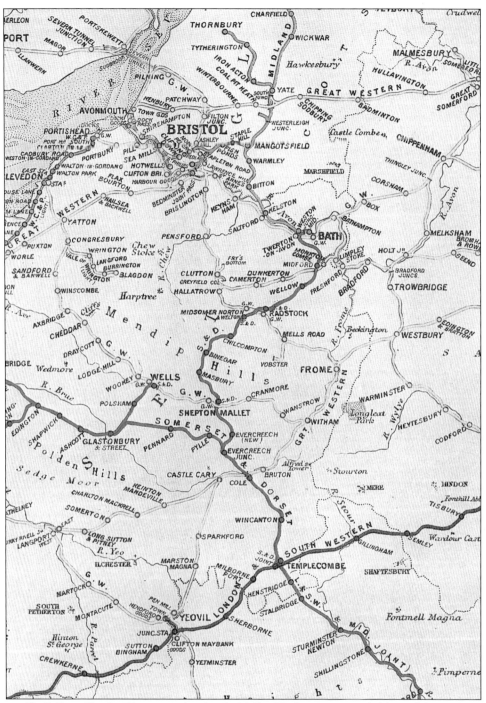

The Railway Clearing House map showing the Midland Railway's Mangotsfield to Bath line and connections with the Somerset & Dorset Joint Railway leading to a junction with the London & South Western Railway.

Chapter One

A Mangotsfield to Bath Branch is Planned

The broad gauge Bristol & Gloucester Railway opened on 8th July, 1844 completing a chain of rail communication from Newcastle-upon-Tyne to Exeter. As part of its efforts to expand, the Midland Railway took over the Bristol & Gloucester in 1845, the line becoming standard gauge in 1854. Wasting no time, on 2nd May, 1846 the MR gave notice that it intended applying to Parliament for a Bill to construct a line to Bath.

The 9¾ mile-long branch was to start from Mangotsfield station, then just south of the bridge carrying the Pucklechurch road, and proceed to Goose Green where a third leg of the triangular junction would have led back to the Bristol line. From Goose Green the line was to climb for 2¼ miles on a gradient of 1 in 100, passing north of Wick, to a summit at the west portal of Freezing Hill tunnel, 1,518 yds in length, the line continuing to descend for five miles almost to Bath, following the Swainswick Valley. Crossing the London Road at Lambridge, it would have spanned the Avon by two 45 ft openings before reaching a terminus at Bathwick, on the site of the present (2005) fire station. The line's estimated cost was £260,000.

Although the proposal was withdrawn after its second reading in the Commons, the idea was not forgotten. Certainly the *Bath Chronicle* favoured the branch, its leading article of 6th November, 1862 proclaiming:

We have most of us seen the list of places for which the Midland Company advertise week after week, during the summer months, that they are willing to issue excursion tickets. The lakes of Westmoreland, North Wales, Scotland and Ireland have been presented before us as possible sights; and many have doubtless planned a summer trip to each in turn. The good fathers of Bath, however, have hitherto had considerable difficulty in doing anything more than read these tempting programmes of excursions to spots of famous scenery. First of all the tickets advertised can only be obtained at Bristol, then it is necessary to start from Bath at 7.15 am if the traveller aspires to catch the express train for the North; and if he reaches Bristol at the time set down in *Bradshaw*, he would have exactly ten minutes to get the tickets and transfer himself and his baggage to the Northern train. Too often, however, the adventurous traveller arrives at Bristol only to see the train he wished to catch glide gently from the station, and has to undergo, as best he may, two or three hours of the 'waiting room', an extra night on the road, and other advantages consequent on his being just too late. Many of our readers, too, must have had their patience exercised at Bristol by the train from Bath running into one part of the station, then backing and running into another part, in a manner utterly incomprehensible to the uninitiated mind.

In 1862 John Sydney Crossley, the Midland Railway's Engineer, and surveyor Charles R. Cheffins of London, planned a nine mile-long line from Mangotsfield, through Goose Green, Bridge Yate, Upton Cheyney and then paralleling the Bitton to Bath road to Bath where it was to bisect the Lower Common between the Victoria Park and the Upper Bristol Road and run to a terminus at the rear of Queen's Parade. Gradients were easier than those proposed for the 1846 scheme, the ruling gradient being 1 in 100 and only 1½ miles at this inclination. The chief engineering feature was a viaduct, 239 yds in length, in the Golden Valley crossing the River Boyd at a height of 90 ft.

Charles E. Davis, the Bath city architect, reporting to the Freemen & General Purposes Committee and showing care for the environment, said that the line proposed would not interfere with 'any advantages common to the estate, provided the embankment was planted with ornamental trees and shrubs as it would then form a screen between the Park and the very ragged buildings in the Lower [sic] Bristol Road always however providing the company undertake to burn nothing but coke in their locomotives as coal smoke would seriously damage the shrubs in the Park'. The MR proposed to reserve the power to occupy the whole of the freemen's property below the park as a terminus in the event of the Queen's Parade site being rejected. The latter was quite likely because of it being considered detrimental to the properties in the Marlborough Buildings/Queen's Parade areas. Davis observed: 'The erection of such a building would destroy not only the privacy of the Park, but its chief beauties, for not to mention the annoyance of whistling, there would be the shunting and the banging of a goods train. I have never yet seen a station however beautiful in itself that would not be a sad eyesore in this particular locality'.

To obviate this problem, in February 1863 the City Council suggested that a junction be made with the GWR outside the city, at, say, Saltford, and MR trains work over the GWR to Bath. The GWR would not have found this proposal acceptable as its cramped station was quite incapable of handling extra traffic. In January 1863 Samuel Beale, the MR Chairman, wrote to the mayor saying that his company had decided to postpone applying to Parliament until the 1864 Session, but hoped that by approaching Bath by a different route, the company could reduce the amount of works and consequently the period required for construction and so no time would be lost in opening the line.

In November 1863 the Bristol & North Somerset Railway's Bath extension was suggested. With Benjamin Piercy and J.G. Fraser as Engineers, it was proposed to extend the authorised Camerton branch through Priston and follow Newton Brook to Newton Mill where the line was to bifurcate, one branch joining the GWR west of Twerton tunnel, while the other was to cross the river and run to a terminus at James Street, almost on the site of the later Green Park station.

Meanwhile on 5th October, 1863 at a Somerset & Dorset Railway (S&D) meeting at Shepton Mallet, it was stated that the MR had abandoned its intention of having a station near Queen's Parade and would be seeking a line entering the city at a lower level. From Mangotsfield, passing through Warmley and Bitton, it was to follow the Avon valley crossing the river six times, to a terminus at Seymour Street, where nine houses comprising the west side of the road were to be demolished to allow room for the station frontage. The other side of Seymour Street survived until its destruction by German bombs in World War II. The coal depot, being thought unsightly, was planned across the other side of the river away from dwellings.

As property at Bath adjacent to the river was subject to severe flooding after prolonged rain or a thaw of snow, the inhabitants believed that the construction of a railway embankment would exacerbate this trouble as it would prevent floods spreading laterally and they would be deeper in consequence. Additionally, bridge abutments would narrow the river to its ordinary width and increase flooding. The city engineer, investigating the matter, said that the MR line would not 'prejudice the interests of the city', but suggested that instead of the bridges having three arches each of 50 ft, the centre arch be 80 ft and those on either side reduced in proportion. At the beginning of February 1864 the Council intended petitioning against the Bill, but the Mayor persuaded the Council to reconsider the matter and said that most people wanted 'to obtain an extension of the Midland Railway to Bath, with as little inconvenience as possible to the inhabitants and wish as many advantages as could be gained'.

The town clerk and city engineer met the Midland's Chairman, Directors and Engineer on 19th February, 1864 and were assured that the bridge piers would not be masonry, but iron cylinders which were narrower and would offer less resistance to flood water. It was probable that at the same time they offered to replace the three masonry spans with two larger ones of wrought iron.

When the subject of flooding was raised again in November 1867, the MR cunningly proved by statistics that its bridges were to be wider than existing bridges, but ignored criticism that an embankment would prevent a flood spreading.

MR Bridge No. 5 (Locksbrook)	*ft*	
Gross span from abutment to abutment	197	
Deduct space occupied by piles, 2 rows, each 2 ft 6 in.	5	
Net clear run	192	
Parliamentary authorised space	150	
Authorised space exceeded by	42	

MR Bridge No. 6 (near the terminus)	*ft*	
Gross span between abutments	156	
Deduct river piles, 2 rows, each 2 ft 6 in.	5	
	151	
Authorised Parliamentary width	150	
Authorised width exceeded by	1	

Dredge's Bridge (Victoria Suspension)	*ft*	*in.*
Gross span between abutments	139	3
Deduct projecting wall of timber wharf premises walled	18	0
	121	3

The approach road on the Twerton side of this bridge prevents water passing during time of flood.

Motley's Bridge (Windsor)	*ft*
River span	112
Side spans each 51 ft	102
Gross total	214
Northern side space unusable for passage of flood water therefore deduct	51
Net clear run for floodwater	163

Comparison:

Clear waterway

	ft	in.
Bridge No. 5	192	0
Bridge No. 6	151	0
Dredge's	121	3
Motley's	163	0

The Corporation prepared two draft petitions: one in favour and one against. The former observed that the GWR was on the broad gauge (mixed gauge did not reach Bath until June 1874) and that a change of gauge was necessary to places off the broad gauge; that the route to the North was circuitous and that in addition to offering a direct route to passengers, the proposed line 'would also open to your Petitioners the large Coalfields in the North of England and afford them the means of obtaining therefrom at a reasonable cost a plentiful supply of house Coal of good quality'. Regarding street alterations proposed in the Bill the city was 'most desirous that such improvements should be sanctioned'.

The other petition, against the line, and not sent, complained that Chapel Row was barely sufficient for existing traffic and would have been unable to cope with additional traffic to and from the MR station; that the span of the river bridges should be increased to guard against flooding and finally that the Preamble to the Bill was 'untrue and incapable of proof'.

Lt Col W. Inigo Jones of Kelston Park was understandably against the new route as it ran only 150 yds from his home and he already had the GWR only 400 yds distant. In a letter to *The Times* published 5th April, 1864 he said that to avoid legal expenses he had agreed to the Midland's proposition to go through his park, accepting a certain bonus additional to the purchase of land, provided the line kept 400 yds from his house.

Curiously enough, on 30th June as the House of Lords' Committee was discussing the Bath extension, W.G. Grace, then aged 15, first played for the All-England Eleven against the Eighteen of Lansdown and this match took place on Sydenham Field, later to become the site of the Midland's Goods Depot at Bath. Grace wrote, 'I batted sixth man, which I consider rather a high compliment in so strong a team, and was on for over half an hour while I made 15. Just when I got set, an unfortunate mistake of Lillywhite's caused me to be run out'. (Lansdown Cricket Club purchased a new ground at Combe Park in 1865 and, after it had been prepared, used it for the 1867 season.) The Mangotsfield & Bath Act, 27 & 28 Vict. cap. 164, received Royal Assent on 21st July, 1864.

In November the Bristol & North Somerset Railway put forward a scheme similar to that of the previous year, except that instead of running to Bath, the branch north of Twerton tunnel was planned to join the now authorised Midland Railway near Rudmore Farm. This scheme proved abortive.

Chapter Two

Construction

Unfortunately Minute books and local newspapers give little information about construction of the line. The MR Civil Engineer J.S. Crossley reported to the Bath & Thornbury Construction Committee on 31st October, 1864 that the permanent survey was making rapid progress, while the Bath Gas Light & Coke Company was on the verge of applying for powers to build a branch from its works on the Upper Bristol Road and to acquire land over which the Midland possessed powers. Crossley believed this spur needed amending since it was not 'judiciously designed'. Permitted by the Act, negotiations were made for the purchase of the Avon & Gloucestershire Railway (AGR), a horse-worked tramway whose route could have been used between Mangotsfield and Bitton, but negotiations fell through, probably because the line was owned by the GWR which would not have wished to facilitate the Midland's progress into its territory.

The end of May 1865 saw the centre line staked out from Mangotsfield as far as Saltford. Cottrell & Spackman of Bath were appointed land valuers for the usual terms of £30 per mile as far as 9 miles 4 furlongs (the position of the later Bath Junction) and 1½ per cent of the purchase money on the remainder, which involved the buying of many small properties and was much more work. The task of staking the centre was completed by the end of July and the side widths were being proceeded with. It was decided to appoint a local architect to design Bath station. Only a few firms were invited to tender for the construction of the branch. In August, apart from Thompson and Lawson who declined, the following tenders for making the earthworks were received:

	£	s.	d.
(Crossley, the Engineer's estimate	95,565	0	0)
Eckersley & Bayliss	104,000	0	0
Ritson	147,427	14	1
T. Brassey & Co.	118,655	2	0
James Rennie & Co.	133,029	15	7
Joseph Firbank	133,348	10	8
Waring Bros	126,684	12	3
Thomas Oliver	110,466	17	2

Messrs Eckersley & Bayliss won the contract.

They started on the large cutting at Bitton in November 1865 before receiving the official go-ahead, the work being carried out at the contractors' risk since purchase of land had not been completed. The youths of the district succumbed to the temptation to ride on the contractors' wagons. One day when the watchman was absent, lads unchained and unbraked the wagons and enjoyed a half-mile downhill ride. In May 1866 Eckersley & Bayliss were employing 85 artisans, 554 labourers and excavators and 62 horses. In September when wet weather slowed work, 702 men and 65 horses were at work. The following

March saw 443,276 cubic yds completed out of 750,000. Fencing was nearly finished, while excavations had been carried out for four of the river bridges. A consequence of changing the spans of all the river bridges was an increased weight of wrought iron and a decrease in cast-iron work. It was found necessary to make the bridge near Bath station wide enough for four tracks in order to give sufficient length to the station, the station throat having to be placed west of the river crossing.

Little progress was made from June to September thanks to a sub-contractor disagreeing with Messrs Eckersley & Bayliss and withdrawing, while in December Crossley complained that earthworks were not proceeding as rapidly as they should, only 13,600 cubic yds being completed as against the possible 30,000. 'With great exertion the line may be finished in July or August, but much will depend upon the weather in the Winter.' The abutments and piers of all the river bridges were complete, while Messrs Handyside & Co. of Derby who were responsible for the bridges had erected girders over four. Eckersley & Bayliss had excavated for the foundations of Bath station and were laying down Pennant rubble to formation level.

Crossley's estimate			Accepted tender	
£	£			
Bath station		9,535	Charles Humphries, Derby	9,539
Bath station roof		6,028	Messrs Handyside, Derby	6,086

Humphries also won the contracts for building Weston and Kelston stations, Samuel Robertson being given those for Bitton and Warmley. Although each station varied, Bitton's prices were typical, Robertson erecting the passenger station for £1,326 9s. 9d. and the goods shed for an additional £628 10s. 0d.

In May 1866 navvies employed on building the line at Saltford and Kelston were invited to the Working Men's Hall, Saltford where 'an excellent tea, with beef, ham and plum cake' was provided by Colonel Inigo Jones of Kelston Park and Miss Drury of Saltford. Following the meal, the Colonel urged all the men to avoid going to the public house and use instead the hall fitted up by Miss Drury as a reading room for them. July 1867 saw houses in Albert Buildings (set at right angles to Victoria Buildings which still exists in the Lower Bristol Road, Bath) already in the contractors' hands, while other residents received 21 days' notice to give up their homes.

In March 1868 it was decided that Mangotsfield station be moved southwards from the North Junction to a new site at Rodway Hill in order to be on the route of Bath to Bristol trains. The following June it was agreed that a station should be built at Warmley instead of at North Common, which would have been midway between Mangotsfield and Bitton.

By the end of March 1869 the permanent way had been completed on one line from Bath goods yard to Mangotsfield, the other line only lacking a mile of track. Crossley observed that the permanent way was far from good and said he had drawn the contractors' attention to its unsatisfactory state. Three locomotives and 500 men were at work on ballasting. The walls of Bath station were erected, the iron work for the roof delivered, columns set up and three of the wrought-iron ribs set in place. The planking of the platforms was in progress. Work on Weston station had not started, but the ground had been prepared and the level crossing gate lodge built - in the event this became the station master's house. It was anticipated that work on Kelston station would be started immediately and completed within a month. Bitton station was almost complete, while at Warmley matters were well in hand and the level crossing lodge and station house completed. Work had begun on the new Mangotsfield station.

In April fireman Pullen was badly injured. While near Bitton he saw a stone on the line and thinking it might cause a derailment, jumped down and removed it. In climbing back on the footplate his foot slipped and he fell, the engine passing over and fracturing a leg beside causing other injuries. He was conveyed to the Royal United Hospital at Bath.

At the end of May, Crossley reported that the line was complete and in good order; works on stations were almost ready for passengers; the locomotive shed was being erected at Bath and the turntable pit was ready to receive the rest. Bath passenger station building was finished and the train shed roof in an advanced stage while tenders had been received for erecting a goods shed at Bath. Charles Humphries' tender of £4,300 was accepted, Crossley's estimate being £4,620. In mid-June four locomotives were coupled together and run across the bridges in order to test their deflection under load.

Colonel Yolland inspected the line on 28th July, 1869, making the following report on 2nd August:

Sir,

I have the honor [sic] to report for the information of the Board of Trade that in obedience to your minute of the 22nd ult., I inspected on the 20th ult., the Mangotsfield and Bath Branch of the Midland Railway, which commences at a Junction with the Gloucester and Bristol Line at Mangotsfield and terminates at Bath, a length of 10 miles and 13 chains.

This branch is double throughout. The width at formation level is 27 feet in Cuttings, and 33 feet on Embankments. The Gauge is 4 feet 8½ inches, and the space between Lines 6 feet. The permanent way consists of a double headed rail that weighs 80 lbs per yard in lengths of 20 feet, fixed in Cast iron Chairs, that each weigh 34 lbs, by means of wooden Keys placed inside the rails. The chairs are fixed by twisted Iron Spikes to transverse sleepers of Baltic Timber, 9 feet long, by 10 inches x 5 inches (rectangular), placed 3 feet apart from centre to centre, except at the joints where they are 2 feet apart. The joints of the Rails are fished in the usual manner.

The Ballast is of broken stone, ashes and gravel and stated to be 1 foot deep, below the under sides of the Sleepers.

The steepest gradient on the Line is 1 in 120, and the sharpest curve has a radius of 30 chains.

There are 13 over and 17 under Bridges, besides 7 Viaducts six of which are over the River Avon.

Most of the over bridges are constructed of stone, and also about one half of the under Bridges, the remainder have stone abutments and wrought or cast iron Girders. One of the Viaducts is built entirely of stone, the others have stone abutments, are of 2 spans, with cast iron pillars in the centre, and wrought iron Lattice Girders - these vary from 71¼ to 102¾ feet spans. The Masonry in the bridges and Viaducts appears to be standing well, but is not of first rate quality: the iron work is good - the girders are sufficiently strong by calculation, and in the large openings, the deflections under a rolling load were moderate. The Viaduct nearest to Bath is for 4 Lines of way.

There are 5 Stations on the Line, Warmley, Bitton, Saltford, Weston and Bath. Saltford is a private Station for the Proprietor of the adjacent Land, who has to make a road to it. There are no Station buildings and the Platforms are incomplete. It is not intended to be used at the present time, except as a Telegraph Station. [Kelston, as it became known, eventually opened as a public station, but there was never any road access.]

An Engine Turntable has been provided at Bath Station, and I am informed that Traffic is to be worked through from Bristol to Bath and back and not by a separate Engine from Mangotsfield.

The permanent way on the Line is in good order, but there have been a few serious slips in the embankments and these will require to be attended to when the wet weather sets in. The post and rail fencing along the Line is by no means good, and does not appear to be equal to the Company's specification. In consequence, it will the sooner require repair. The wooden Keys supplied out of the Company's Stores are indifferent. When I went over the Line there were some few things still remaining to be done.

1. Thus at Bath, the Glazing of the Roof was incomplete - Buffer stops remained to be put up and the Points and Signals were not all connected together. Short trains could be worked from under a portion of the roof when the Glazing had been finished.
2. At Weston, the down distant signal could not be seen from the Station and an Electric Repeater was to be put up.
3. At Saltford, a cross over Road was to be taken out, and the switches spiked and removed.
4. At Bitton Station, an Electric Repeater for a distant Signal that could not be seen was to be supplied and a similar want occurred at Warmley Station. The coping of the Platform was incomplete.
5. Blind sidings are required, 2 at Bath, 2 at Weston, 1 at Bitton and 1 at Warmley Stations.
6. The Locking required to be improved or completed at Bath and at the East [South] and North Junctions at Mangotsfield.

I have however since received the enclosed letter from Mr Crossley stating that all these requirements have been attended to or are in process of being completed.

Bitton Station is situated on an Incline of 1 in 120, which extends for a mile below this Station. Safety Switches placed on the Line to Mangotsfield, immediately below the Platform are necessary, if the Traffic were to be worked in the ordinary manner and not on the Absolute Block System - but they may be dispensed with, in consequence of the Company undertaking to work on the Absolute Block System, and that the next Telegraph Station from Bitton towards Bath is at Saltford - so that if a Train were to break loose at Bitton, and run down the Incline it would, in consequence of having to run 26 chains on the Level, and 35 chains up an Ascending gradient of 1 in 264, come to a stand still, before reaching Saltford.

There are 2 authorised Level Crossings on this Branch: one is that of an important Turnpike Road and the other of a Public Road. Temporary Gates are erected at the Turnpike Road to be replaced by iron gates which are to be opened simultaneously. In both instances mechanical arrangements should be introduced to prevent the Gates from being opened for the Road Traffic, except when the Signals in both directions are at danger.

I recommend that the sanction of the Board of Trade for the opening of the Line between Mangotsfield and Bath may be given.

Chapter Three

Opening

On 3rd August, 1869, the day prior to the opening of the line, there were the makings of a disaster when a workman at Bath station caused an explosion as he applied a light to gas escaping from a poorly jointed pipe. Although the blast was strong enough to blow out windows and force a door off its hinges, fortunately no one was injured.

The line opened to passenger traffic on 4th August, the *Bath Chronicle* reporting:

> The event was unattended by ceremony, and, except that Mr J. Stone's porter stores, at the bottom of Charles Street, were adorned with flags and a scroll wishing 'Success to the Midland Railway', there was no outward display to show that anything particular was going on.
>
> The first train was timed to leave Bath at 7.40, but long before that hour people began to assemble in and about the station. The train, consisting of a powerful engine, nine carriages (four third class, and all new, the second class coaches being most comfortably padded) and a carriage truck on which was a small phaeton. The third class carriages were soon filled, not to say crowded, and the first and second were also patronised. The majority of the passengers went, simply for the purpose of saying that they travelled in the first train on a new line, and booked only to Weston - a penny ride. At 7.48 the guard gave the signal, and the train quietly glided out of the station, the passengers getting up a faint cheer. At five minutes past eight o'clock a train from Bristol (due at 7.55) came in, and with it a great number of those who had left Bath a little more than a quarter of an hour previously. Much has yet to be done to render the station complete.

To encourage traffic to develop, from 26th August return market tickets to Bristol were issued for the first three trains. One of the first excursion trains from Bath left at 5.30 am on 30th September for the Birmingham Great Onion Fair. In November the Midland acceded to a request from Bath and Bristol sportsmen that hunting tickets be granted at single fare for a return journey. In September 1872 the *Bath Chronicle* reported that 'A richly decorated and furnished saloon carriage has been secured for the use of Bath travellers from the Midland Station in this city. The use of the carriage can be secured by taking six or more first class tickets for a party'. Passenger traffic developed to such an extent that by April 1870 the platforms at Bath had to be extended for 240 ft on the departure side and 120 ft on the other side, while a carriage dock was made at the rear of the arrival platform.

As the goods shed and coal wharves were yet to be completed and the Bath Gas Company had not yet connected its works with the MR, goods and mineral traffic did not start until 1st September, 1869, though on this date the goods shed still was not ready. The *Bath Chronicle*, unusually for a local paper, devoted quite a few inches of space describing the goods shed. Its edition for 10th March, 1870 reported:

MIDLAND RAILWAY.

OPENING OF THE LINE TO

BATH.

The BATH and MANGOTSFIELD Extension of the Midland Railway, will be opened on

WEDNESDAY, AUGUST 4th, 1869,

Affording a new and direct route between BATH and GLOUCESTER, WORCESTER, BIRMINGHAM, and the whole of the Midland System, also a new and convenient route between BATH and BRISTOL.

Thro' Trains will run between BRISTOL and BATH, and be in connection at MANGOTSFIELD with Main Line Trains to and from BIRMINGHAM and the NORTH as under:

This Table shows the Times at which the Trains may be expected to arrive at and depart from the several Stations, but their arrival at the times stated is not guaranteed, nor does the Company hold itself responsible for delay or any consequences arising therefrom.

[Detailed timetable showing stations including BATH, Weston, Kelston, Saltford, MANGOTSFIELD, Yate, Berkeley Road, Dursley, Stonehouse, Stroud, GLOUCESTER, Chepstow, Newport, Cardiff, Carmarthen Junction, New Milford, CHELTENHAM, Tewkesbury, WORCESTER, BIRMINGHAM, Leicester, Peterboro', Cambridge, Burton, Derby, Matlock, Nottingham, Newark, Lincoln, Sheffield, MANCHESTER via Matlock, Liverpool, York, Scarboro', Newcastle, Leeds, Bradford, GLASGOW, etc., with Week-Days and Sundays train times and Fares from Bath]

TRAINS BETWEEN BRISTOL AND BATH.

BATH TO BRISTOL.

[Timetable: Week-Days and Sundays. Stations: BATH, Weston, Kelston, Saltford, Fish Ponds, BRISTOL. Fares from Bath.]

BRISTOL TO BATH.

[Timetable: Week-Days and Sundays. Stations: BRISTOL, Fish Ponds, MANGOTSFIELD, Warmley, Kelston, Weston, Bath.]

THROUGH THIRD CLASS ARRANGEMENTS.

No. 2 is Third Class from Bath to Stations between Mangotsfield and Gloucester, and Stations North of Gloucester.

No. 6 is Third Class from Bath to Stations between Mangotsfield and Birmingham.

No. 18 is Third Class from Birmingham and intermediate Stations to Bath.

No. 22 is Third Class from Stations enumerated to Bath.

JAMES ALLPORT, General-Manager.

The opening timetable for the Bath & Mangotsfield extension.

The facade of Bath MR station *c.*1870.   *Author's Collection*

The interior of Bath MR station *c.*1870, view from the buffer stops. Staff on the arrival platform await a train. A 6-wheel passenger coach stands on a centre carriage road.

M.J. Tozer Collection

Bitton bridge over the Avon. This 1876 engraving appeared in *The Midland Railway: Its Rise and Progress* by F.S. Williams. A photograph of its replacement can be seen on page 50.

Weston bridge over the Avon situated nearly a mile west of Weston station. The New Bridge, which now carries the A4, is in the background. This is another print from Williams' book.

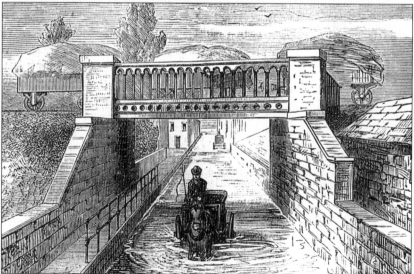

The flooded Victoria Bridge Road under the MR main line at Bath, 1875. This road had to be lowered when the railway was built.

Illustrated London News

Possessing as it does facilities for the acquirement of an extensive business in the transit of commercial produce to and from one of the richest districts in the kingdom, it is not surprising that the Midland Railway Company should be animated with a spirit of enterprise in the conduct of their affairs, and in the provision of all the accessories necessary to the extension of their business. To this circumstance must be attributed the efforts which have resulted in the erection of the Company's new Goods Station in Sydenham-field, now rapidly approaching completion. Hitherto the Company have had a large goods business in this city, but the facilities for its conduct have been considerably curtailed by the absence of a proper goods station. The building now in the course of erection, is, we imagine, in every way likely to support the want, and both in point of position, and in the mode of its construction, will be found to answer the purpose very satisfactorily. Sydenham-field being considerably below the level of the line, the permanent way has of necessity been laid down on an embankment running through it, and the works in connection with this have been somewhat extensive in character, about 200 navvies being now engaged upon it.

As access to the goods and coal yard was from the Lower Bristol Road and no direct street led to the passenger station and the city centre, traffic was forced to go half a mile along the Lower Bristol Road to the Old Bridge in order to cross the river and then travel the same distance back. To obviate this unnecessary mileage, the Midland promised to provide a new bridge. Again quoting from the *Chronicle*:

The bridge will be of cast iron, and in most respects similar to the existing one, [i.e. the railway bridge] with which it will be parallel at a distance of about a hundred yards. It will, however, differ from the other in that it will have no piers to support it in the centre. The bridge will have a clear span of 150 feet, while its width will be 24 feet. The abutments on the Seymour-street side of the river are now in course of construction, and the form and appearance of this important part of the work seem to warrant the supposition that the general formation of the bridge will be of an attractive and enduring character. Two roads to the goods station are being constructed, the one leading from Seymour-street and crossing the bridge, and the other from the Lower Bristol-road. The former has a gradient of one in thirty, and the other of one in twenty-five. We understand that the latter road will be completed and ready for use in about a month, and the road over the bridge in three months. The result of the work, so enterprisingly embarked on by the Company, and so admirably carried out by Mr Humphreys [*sic*], of Derby, and his manager, Mr Green, from the plans of Messrs Allport, jun., and Wilson, the engineers, and the architect, Mr Saunders, is that the most perfect facilities have been obtained for conducting an extensive goods traffic to and from the city; and we have no doubt that in this department of their business here, the Company will meet with a success corresponding to that of their passenger traffic, which, we hear, has fully answered the high expectations formed of it. The parcels business has been energetically pursued and we have been informed that so favourable have been the results in this matter that the Company contemplate opening a parcels receiving office in the centre of the city.

On 28th April, 1870 the *Bath Chronicle* reported that the abutments of the road bridge were finished:

. . . the upper part of the stonework being covered with a stone (hewn at Matlock we believe) of an unusually substantial nature. Upon this the ironwork will be placed, and as this, which is being supplied by Messrs Butler & Pitt, of Stanningley, near Leeds, is daily expected, the work will soon go on uninterruptedly, until its completion. The bridge will be of 150 feet span, on stone abutments, sunk 20 feet into the earth. Its width will be 24 feet, corresponding with that of the road leading to it. About halfway between the two bridges the company contemplate constructing a large steam crane, which will be used for the purpose of unloading stone, coal, and other goods from barges in the river below. [It is believed this was never constructed.] In the other direction, at the side of the roadway leading from the Bristol-road, a ponderous weighing machine for carts and heavy purposes is fitted up, and further on, near the gate, there is a row of offices (six in number), erected with the intention of being let by the Company to merchants and others. One point in connection with the Company's goods traffic remains to be noted, and that is, they intend to conduct their own collecting here, and with this object an adequate stud of horses has been provided, stables being erected at the commencement of the road in Seymour-street, in close proximity to the passenger station.

Speaking generally, the works which have been carried out appear to be of a most satisfactory character, and point to an enterprising spirit on the part of the Company. So far as Bath is concerned they have every facility for conducting a large and remunerative business in the transit of goods. We may add that Mr Brooks, the present manager at the passenger station, will also take the management of the goods department.

The bridge link with the goods yard was not opened quite as soon as anticipated, it being recorded that, in September, work on the bridge was delayed by girders falling sideways when being launched. As this bridge was owned and built by the Midland, it was opened to the public by courtesy only, a pair of gates at each end of the approach road being closed at 11 pm.

Because the Midland had placed its passenger station in an area of the city where land was inexpensive, it was prepared to lay out money to make it more accessible. Chapel Row, *en route* to Queen Square and the high class residential areas of the city, was narrow and required widening which led to litigation. The Reverend T. Loughnan claimed compensation for the loss of his proprietory chapel, St Mary's, which the MR had acquired under its Act for the purposes of street improvement. The Reverend Loughnan's witnesses put compensation at £7,568 and £7,984, while those of the Midland opted for £1,800 and £2,794. The arbitrator, Mr Charles Pollock QC, awarded £4,150. Stones from the chapel together with surplus land were sold for £3,000 to the builders of St Paul's (now Holy Trinity) Church. The Elephant & Castle Inn, Monmouth Place, also had to be purchased and demolished by the MR.

Another road improvement was the cutting of a fresh thoroughfare, New Street, between James Street and Kingsmead Square to give direct access from the station to the city centre. When completed, Chapel Row and New Street were maintained by the Corporation.

Some folk cared for the environment, permission being granted in October 1869 for the Reverend W.E. Ray to plant the slopes opposite his house at Bitton on agreeing to pay five shillings per annum by way of acknowledgement. The company said it would not be liable for any damage occurring to plants by fire or otherwise.

Chapter Four

Consolidation

The Midland Bridge was only wide enough for a single carriageway and because of loose rivets, corroded plates and limited carrying capacity, Francis Campin, past president of the Civil & Mechanical Engineers' Society, in an undated report said it was 'absolutely unfitted' for its position and was a source of danger. When, on 18th September, 1903, a Light Railway Order was granted for Bath Electric Tramways to run a route from Kingsmead Square to the Lower Bristol Road via the Midland Bridge, the tramways company agreed to pay two-thirds of the cost of a replacement bridge with 164 ft span and 36 ft width. Although the tramway paid, its cars never used the bridge, trams not being allowed to run down Westgate Street as the company had planned. Rails had been laid on the bridge itself to avoid disturbing the new road surface if the line was required. (For more information see *Bath Tramways* by Colin Maggs, published by Oakwood Press.) Messrs Handyside won the contract to build the bridge, which opened on 12th December, 1905, the former bridge being purchased from Messrs Handyside by the city council and moved downstream to form the Destructor Bridge where it still stands.

Bus competition began to make itself felt in 1931 when on 18th June the Traffic Commissioners considered whether a licence should be granted for a Bath-Bristol service via Bitton, a route which roughly paralleled the railway. The hourly bus service, jointly operated by the Bristol Tramways & Carriage Company and Bath Electric Tramways Company and commenced in 1928, had developed to such an extent that four times the number of passengers travelled from Bath to Bristol via Bitton by bus than used rail. Kelston Parish Council observed that the village station was ¾ mile across muddy fields, while Bitton station was ¾ mile from the village centre. The Traffic Commissioners believed that rail and bus services were both remunerative and granted a bus licence.

Until 1931 hop-pickers had travelled to Ledbury by lorry, but on 1st September, 70 left Bath on the 7.25 am train, travelling in a special coach, a separate van containing their luggage. On 30th July, 1934, 1,292 children travelled from Bath to Clifton Down in two trains, each double-headed. This special excursion to Bristol Zoo was paid for by the Sportsmen's Outing to Poor Children.

The chief feature of the 1930s was the bridge rebuilding programme. The lattice work bridges would not support anything larger than a class '3P' 4-4-0 and were becoming life expired, a train crossing them causing a vertical movement of the piers. Although thoughts were first raised in 1923, plans were held in abeyance until 1932 when the replacement cost was estimated to be £99,200, but in the event this figure rose to nearly £140,000. Fortunately the project was completed just prior to World War II when the line became highly strategic, conveying British and Allied troops together with supplies to the south coast for the Normandy invasion. Initially the road underbridges were replaced. On Sunday 27th August, 1933 a crane tipped as it was lifting a 5 ton cast-iron bridge girder at the junction of Rudmore Park and Brassmill Lane, Bath and the girder crashed to the road. As it had snapped the wires of the railway telephone system, a message was sent to Bath Police Station which in

Station staff by the porte-cochère, 1914.   *Author's Collection*

Bristol Tramways fleet of taxis at Bath *c.*1922. They are De Dion Bouton cars with radiators at the rear of the bonnet.   *Rupert Spurrell Collection*

The Bath branch of the Amalgamated Society of Railway Servants, England, Ireland, Scotland & Wales outside Royal Oak, Lower Bristol Road, Bath *c*.1913. *Author's Collection*

German prisoners-of-war at Bath, February 1917.

Author's Collection

Station master Arthur Exton poses on the departure platform at Bath *c*.1928. A horse-drawn van stands in the stable yard beyond.

Mrs E.K. Holten

The original Midland Bridge left, and its replacement on the far right, seen here in 1905.
Author's Collection

The maker's plate on the new Midland Bridge, with the railway bridge in the top right-hand
corner of the picture.   *Author*

turn telephoned the GWR at Bristol to send its breakdown crane to the rescue. A messenger cycled to Bitton to warn the signalman to let the train through. GWR steam crane No. 1 was hauled by a GWR '55XX' 2-6-2 tank engine, the first time a GWR locomotive had used the line. Rail traffic was halted until re-opened about 10 pm, passengers being carried to Bitton by bus.

The first contract for replacing or strengthening the six large river bridges with spans varying from 75 to 106 ft was placed in 1933. The superstructure of five of these bridges was replaced with new steel girders and floors of steel and concrete. The sixth bridge, a four-road structure outside Bath station which was only traversed at low speeds, was strengthened by Walters Engineering Ltd, Bath, welding every joint, 23rd to 25th July, 1937, because renewal of this bridge would have caused too much chaos to traffic. The central piers consisting of 10 cast-iron columns or screw piles were replaced by new concrete piers at all six bridges.

S.G. Thompson of the London Midland & Scottish Railway (LMS) engineering staff was in charge of the work which started with the river bridge No. 35 just west of Rudmore Park. The operation was the same as at subsequent bridges. The section between Weston and Bitton was split to make two 'blocks', a temporary signal box 'Rudmore Park' being erected 110 yds west of the bridge. This controlled traffic by upper quadrant signals (the first in the district) on the single line over the bridge, which was replaced in two halves. One road remained in use as a running line, the other becoming a temporary siding for storing girders awaiting erection. These latter, weighing up to 83 tons each, arrived on bogies, the girders themselves connecting them. Steel columns supported the river ends of the main girders while the concrete pier was built. To form this central pier, a coffer dam was erected round the old cast-iron columns, a man in a rowing boat stopping leaks by tipping out clay which was washed into the leak rendering it water tight. Following the removal of the old columns, the new pier was built.

The *Bath Chronicle* said that the process of launching a girder was slow 'in fact, barely perceptible. It was a stately, but not a spectacular operation'. When in position, the girder was lowered to the pier and abutments. For this purpose a steel gantry was erected on the central and side girders of the original bridge. It was hoped that the platforms built for unloading bridge material would be left to serve as a halt for the locality, but the LMS did not do this, believing that Bath Electric Tramways offered too much competition. When a new bridge was completed, the temporary signal box was moved to a new location at the next bridge to be replaced.

By early November 1937 the Boyd-Avon bridge east of Bitton had been completed and only the bridge west of Kelston remained to be dealt with. The Engineer's Department gave permission for locomotives up to the weight of a 'Black Five' to work into Bath, subject to a special restriction over Kelston bridge. The use of Compounds and 'Black Fives' enabled some double-heading to be dispensed with. Kelston bridge was replaced in 1939, buses replacing some trains on 27th March and 7th and 14th May to facilitate the work. Buses left Bath at 8.30 am and 9.30 am arriving Bitton 8.42 and 9.41, returning from Bitton at 10.24 and arriving Bath 10.37 am. The 11 to 13 minutes allowed was not generous enough for the 6½ miles of curving, undulating road and the Bitton arrival times for May were eased to 8.48 and 9.48 am, while the down bus schedule was amended to leave Bitton at 10.28, Kelston 10.40 and arrive at Bath 10.46 am. Running sand encountered at Kelston

Ex-LNWR 2-4-0 No. 5014 *Murdoch* with an Engineer's saloon between Warmley and Bitton, 1930. Notice that the locomotive carries a disc, not head lamp.　　*Revd Alan Newman Collection*

COOK'S EASTER EXCURSIONS FROM BATH.

WEDNESDAY, APRIL 8 for return up to 13 days
Londonderry.

THURSDAY, April 9th for return up to 15 days.
North of Ireland.

THURSDAY, April 9th, for 5, 6, 9 or 15 days to
Carlisle and Scottand.

THURSDAY, April 9th, for 6, 8, 10 or 15 days to
Eastern Counties.

THURSDAY, April 9, for 5, 6, 8, 10 or 15 days and on Saturday April 11, for 3, 4, 6, 8 or 15 days to

NORTH of WALES. NORTH of ENGL'ND
LAKE DISTRICT. NORTH-EAST DIST.
NORTH-WEST　MIDLANDS.
DISTRICT.　　BLACKPOOL.

Apply for handbills tickets etc. at the company's station.
H. G. BURGESS, General Manager.

L.M.S.

LONDON, MIDLAND AND SCOTTISH RAILWAY

EASTER HOLIDAY EXCURSIONS.

The L.M.S. Railway Company have arranged an extensive series of excursion bookings from Bath to all parts of England, Scotland and Ireland.
Handbills, tickets and all information may be obtained at the station or the company's city office, 5, Union Street.
Inquiries addressed to the Station Master, L.M.S. Station, Bath, will receive prompt attention.
H. G. BURGESS, General Manager.

CHEAP TRIPS
from BATH, etc.

VILLA v. SPURS
Sat. Jan. 6th—

Bath　8.40 a.m.　2.0 p.m.　Birmingham
　　　　Return 5.40 p.m.　　　11/9

MIDLANDS TRIPS
Sundays, Jan. 7th & 8th—

　　　　　　　Gloucester &
　　　　　　　Cheltenham Birmingham
　　　a.m.
Bath　10.15
Weston 10.20　　**3/6　5/6**
Return Birmingham 8.30, Cheltenham
　　9.30, Gloucester 9.55 p.m.

PANTO TRIP
Sat., Jan. 13th—

　　　　　　　Gloucester &
　　　　　　　Cheltenham Birmingham
　　　a.m.
Bath　11.0
Weston 11.5　　**3/6　5/6**
Return Birmingham 10.45, Cheltenham
　12 Mid., Gloucester 12.15 a.m.

LATE PANTO. TRAIN.
At 10.53 p.m. on Saturdays until Jan. 27th a train will leave Bath L.M.S. for Kelston, Bitton, Warmley, Mangotsfield, Staple Hill and Fishponds.

RAIL TRAVEL
at Pre-War Fares !
ANY DAY :: ANY TRAIN
1d. per mile Tickets.
ASK FOR FARES PROGRAMME.

TRIPS FROM BATH, Etc.

Saturday, March 31st—
　　　　　　　　　　　BLACKPOOL
11.45 p.m. (Friday) ...　...　14/6
　　　Return Central 11.5 p.m.

EASTER MONDAY—

	a.m.	Glo's- ter.	Ch'lt'n ham.	Bir- ming ham.
Bath	11.10	3/6	3/6	5/6
Weston	11.12	3/6	3/6	5/6
Bitton	11.20	3/-	3/6	5/6
Warmley	11.25	3/-	3/-	5/-
Mangotsfield	11.40	3/-	3/-	5/-
Yate	11.50	2/6	3/-	4/6

Return Birmingham 10.45 p.m., Cheltenham 11.45 p.m., Gloucester 11.55 p.m.

EASTER HOLIDAYS

"Summer Tickets" 1d. per mile.
Any Day.　Any Train.　Anywhere.
Available for one month, minimum
2/6 (4/-) first class.
THE RAIL WAY IS BEST !

FULL INFORMATION AT STATIONS
AND AGENCIES.

Left: LMS excursions advertisement, 28th March, 1925.

Above, centre: LMS excursions advertisement, 5th January, 1934.

Above, right: LMS excursions advertisement, 29th March, 1935.

When lifting a girder whilst replacing the overbridge at the junction of Rudmore Park and Brassmill Lane on 27th August, 1933, the crane collapsed through being insufficiently stabilised. The twisted girder can be seen in the road below. *Bath Evening Chronicle*

Weston Bridge being replaced 1934, view downstream. Notice the temporary signal box.
R.R. Perkins

These two photographs were taken in July 1938 when bridge works were sufficiently advanced to allow heavier engines to work to Bath. *Above:* Class '5' 4-6-0 No. 5042 at the head of the incline down to the ex-S&D locomotive shed at Bath. Another class '5' can be seen in the distance, right. *Below:* Class '4' Compound 4-4-0 No. 1001 carriage shunting at Bath.

(Both) Revd Alan Newman

Bridge girders for Kelston or Avon Bridges. *Author's Collection*

Kelston Bridge replacement: view up 26th March, 1939. The temporary signal box can be seen beyond. *Bath Evening Chronicle*

A class '5' 4-6-0 leaving Bath with an up train *c*.1940. Due to the invasion scare, the wording of the running-in board to the left of the bonded stores has been removed.   *Author's Collection*

The LMS Home Guard platoon at Bath station, August 1943.   *John Stamp*

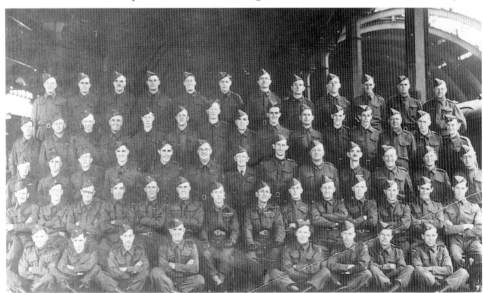

made bridge replacement work difficult, and 56 reinforced concrete piles were required to be driven to form a solid foundation to carry the abutment and wing walls on the western side.

The five years' task of renewing the bridges was completed just in time for the 1939 summer traffic. The 13 bridges rebuilt or strengthened had used 2,750 tons of steel and 8,000 cubic yds of concrete. The temporary signal box used to break the sections was moved to Elm Bridge, where it opened on 29th January, 1940 and split the section between Engine Shed Junction signal box, Gloucester, and Churchdown. Details of the use of this box on the Mangotsfield-Bath line are given below:

Bridge No.	Name of temporary signal box	Opened	Closed
35	Rudmore Park	29.4.34	2.9.34
28	Newton	28.4.35	28.7.35
40	(Frame added to Bath Junction s.b.)		
19	Boyd-Avon	23.5.37	25.7.37
		3.10.37	7.11.37
24	Kelston Bridge	19.3.39	11.6.39

The *Railway Observer* September 1937 p.271 reported that unusual engines had recently appeared at Bath on steam crane workings associated with the replacement of Boyd-Avon bridge included 'Cauliflower' 0-6-0s Nos. 8594 (3C, Walsall), 8619 (17B, Burton) and Kirtley class '1P' 2-4-0 No. 20008 (3C, Walsall).

On several occasions proposals were made for obviating the reversal of through trains at Bath (Green Park) station and to avoid the restrictive single line section Bath to Midford through Devonshire and Combe Down tunnels. It was believed that a connection should be made across Newton Meadows to the GWR and all Bath passenger traffic dealt with at a new station to be built near the GWR's Bath West goods depot. Bournemouth trains would then have been routed via the Bradford-on-Avon line and then the Camerton branch to join the Somerset & Dorset line at Midford. In 1947 the route of the connecting line was actually pegged out across Newton Meadows, where a new locomotive depot was planned.

At one period during World War II, two sets of coaches used on the Somerset & Dorset were taken to Bitton each evening for storage in the goods yard. This was a precaution in case the bridge at Bath station had been bombed, which would have left them marooned. One night, while shunting these coaches at Bitton in the dark, one guard had his legs cut off. An expert in first aid, he instructed the other railwaymen what to do to him as he lay there helpless. After being fitted with artificial limbs he operated the weighbridge at the Midland Goods Depot, Bath. During the Baedeker raids on Bath of 25th, 26th April, 1942 the shed foreman had the foresight to disperse engines to various parts of the yard so that if a bomb fell on the shed damage would be minimised. In the event none were harmed. LMS railwaymen made up a Home Guard platoon at Bath, those who were not members having to undertake fire watching from the top of the goods shed. A plane spotter (whose task it was to ring a bell when hostile aircraft approached) positioned on top of the water softener was once shot at by a German plane, but not hurt. One of the first bombs to fall on Bath dropped on the goods shed causing a fair amount of damage, while several serious fires broke out in the raids of April 1942. The Home Guard patrolled round the yard to ensure that German spies had not altered points so as to derail a train. One enthusiastic Home Guard shot at a railway guard who failed to identify himself when challenged in Bath yard. Fortunately the bullet missed.

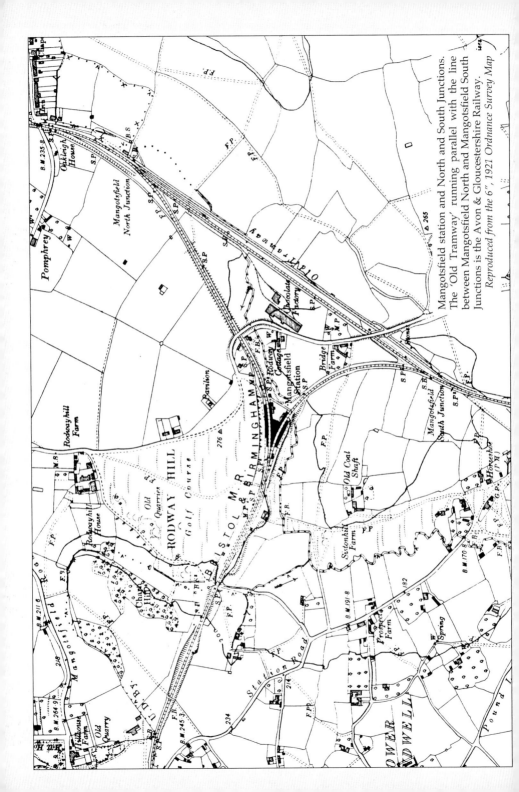

Mangotsfield station and North and South Junctions. The 'Old Tramway' running parallel with the line between Mangotsfield North and Mangotsfield South Junctions is the Avon & Gloucestershire Railway. *Reproduced from the 6", 1921 Ordnance Survey Map*

Chapter Five

Description of the Route

With the opening of the Bath branch, a triangular junction was formed at Mangotsfield, the line from North Junction signal box to South Junction signal box being used by trains to and from Westerleigh goods yard, or Gloucester; the Mangotsfield Station signal box to South Junction signal box spur being used by trains to and from Bristol. Until the opening of the Bath line, the station was at the North Junction, but on 4th August, 1869 was moved south towards Bristol so that it stood at the apex of the junction of the Gloucester and Bath lines from Bristol.

There was an up and down main platform for each line, with an extra down platform for passenger trains running between Mangotsfield and Clifton Down, and an up loop platform on the Gloucester line. These roads were known as 'behind the box' and 'under the rock' respectively, the latter receiving its name from Rodway Hill dominating the station. A tall timber screen protected the station to some extent from the prevailing westerly winds. The platforms were covered by glazed roofing supported by lightweight girders on slender cast-iron columns. The roof was longitudinal in construction, rather than the normal Midland ridge and furrow type, its ends hipped and carrying small finials. The island platforms had timber waiting shelters. The platforms were connected by subway and it is said that when this was being cut c.1900, enough coal was extracted from the outcrop for the labourers to boil their tea. The dark, dank subway inspired the Bath playwright Arnold Ridley to write *The Ghost Train*.

The fact that the station lacked a refreshment room has been explained by the story that the landowner, who also had land on which was sited the nearest hotel, stipulated that the railway could have the land as long as no refreshment facilities were offered. In addition to its use as a junction station, and for passengers to or from Mangotsfield itself, it was also adjacent to Carson's chocolate factory which had a large number of employees, some of whom travelled by rail. The station closed to passengers on 7th March, 1966. Curiously for a principal junction station, it had but one water crane and this was tucked away on a siding by the down main home signal. The staff comprised a station master, two booking clerks, two foremen, three porters on each of the two daily shifts and one night porter. Mangotsfield Station signal box, known as South Junction signal box until 29th October, 1877, was destroyed by fire on 22nd January, 1967 and not replaced, the curve between the station and Mangotsfield South junction being closed on that date. South of the station were engineer's sidings on the down side and a private siding, access to which was given by Mangotsfield Stone Sidings signal box (from 10th December, 1877). This closed on 21st July, 1935.

The two goods sidings at Mangotsfield North were shunted by Bristol crews, these also working Carson's private siding, opened in 1912 as 'Packer's' and closed in 1963. Crews shunting this siding were allowed to purchase chocolates at a reduced rate. The goods depot at Mangotsfield North closed on 10th June, 1963,

Mangotsfield station.

Reproduced from the 25", 1915 Ordnance Survey Map

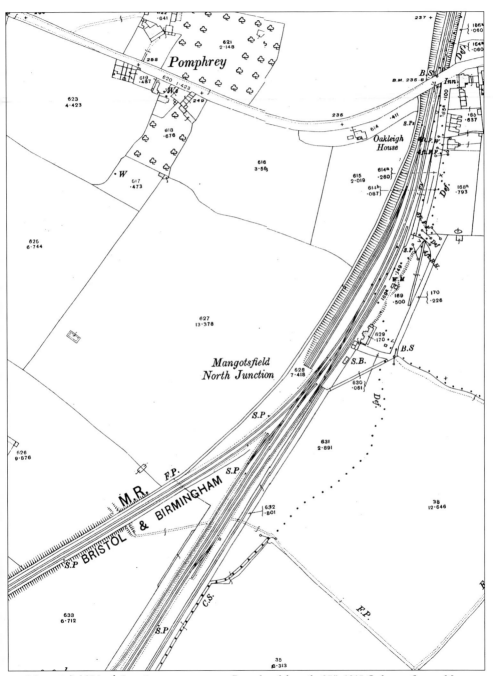

Mangotsfield North Junction.

Reproduced from the 25", 1915 Ordnance Survey Map

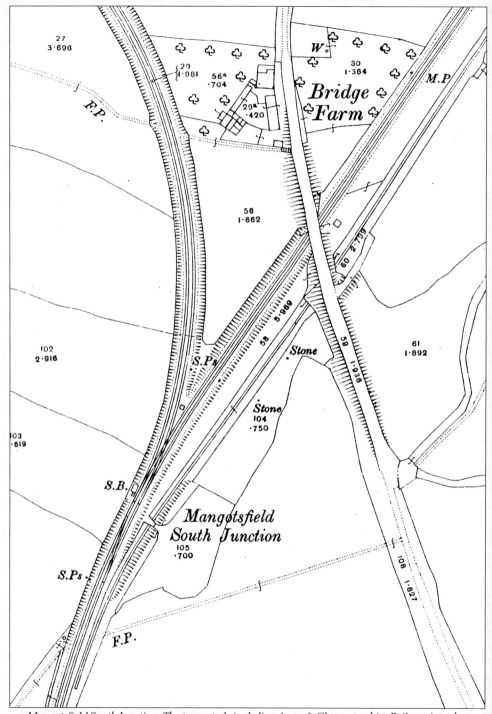

Mangotsfield South Junction. The truncated single line Avon & Gloucestershire Railway is to the east of the double track MR line. *Reproduced from the 25", 1915 Ordnance Survey Map*

The original Mangotsfield station building at Mangotsfield North Junction, 21st April, 1960. In front of the station is a World War II Ministry of Transport wagon. The left-hand section of the building contains the offices of the Mangotsfield Coal Company. Although a coal merchant rented the building, railway fire buckets still hang on the wall. Notice the cattle dock to the left of the signal box.   *Author*

Class '2P' 4-4-0 No. 40700, a class '7F' 2-8-0 and class '4' 2-6-0 No. 43014 having arrived from Bath tender-first to turn on the Mangotsfield triangle when the Bath turntable was under repair, are proceeding to North Junction before returning tender-first to Bath. This view was probably taken in December 1950.   *Downend Historical Society*

Mangotsfield, 20th July, 1935: Gloucester lines in the foreground and the Bath branch platforms beyond. The wind barrier to shelter passengers can be seen in the background.   *Author*

Mangotsfield, 21st April, 1960. Bath platform left and the bay platform, known as 'Behind the box', right. It was formerly used by the Mangotsfield to Clifton Down service until this was withdrawn in World War II.   *Author*

though the old station house remains. The first building was the small one-storey toll house built in 1830 for the Avon & Gloucestershire and Bristol & Gloucestershire railways; the two-storey station house built in 1844 stands alongside it. Opposite the North Junction signal box were three carriage sidings; these were taken out of use on 12th September, 1965, the box itself closing on 3rd January, 1970. In the 1960s rotted window frames were replaced by those of GWR pattern.

A limit of 15 mph was imposed at the North Junction to and from Bath and 65 mph over the whole branch. The Bath line descended at 1 in 180 from the North Junction past Carson's siding towards South Junction, this line not being used by passenger trains after the withdrawal of the 'Pines Express' on 10th September, 1962.

Mangotsfield South Junction signal box ('East Junction' until 29th October, 1877), at the convergence of the lines from the North Junction and the station, closed on 6th October, 1935, this junction then being worked economically from the Station signal box, the signals being classified as intermediate. The Station box dealt with such trains as the 'Pines Express', yet did not actually see them. At the South Junction the line steepened to 1 in 121 down, but became level at Warmley. The Avon & Gloucestershire Railway (see *The Bristol & Gloucester Railway and The Avon & Gloucestershire Railway* by Colin Maggs, published by Oakwood Press) curved round Siston Hill to avoid making a cutting, but when the Midland Railway's Bath branch was built, to avoid crossing the AGR twice on the level, there being insufficient headroom to allow a bridge without seriously interfering with gradients, the AGR was diverted by building a new and more direct line beside and on the east side of the MR. As the Bath branch was not completed until 1869, it is arguable that the AGR was still expecting traffic at that time, as the last entry in its account book was January 1867.

Warmley station (126 miles 9 chains from Derby; 1 mile 43 chains from Mangotsfield North Junction; 1 mile 24 chains from Mangotsfield station) had timber buildings, the main one containing the offices being on the up platform. The building had extended eaves, shallow hipped roofs and round-headed windows. The waiting room on the down platform remains in use as a café for users of the footpath and cycle track which follows the railway formation. North of the waiting shelter on the down platform was a permanent way men's hut. The 1899 footbridge with timber stairs had its lattice work sides boarded by 1912. In addition to giving communication between platforms, this footbridge could also be used by pedestrians when the level crossing gates were shut against them. To this end, access was by staircases from both road and platform. It was replaced by a plate girder footbridge in 1929. About this date a black timber store room was erected on the up platform for parcels awaiting collection. Palm trees grew in the station garden.

The goods yard, with a large brick and stone goods shed, was situated on the up side. It had three roads:

The Front (or Outside) Road leading to the Cattle Pen Road
The Goods Shed (or Middle) Road
The Long (or Back) Road

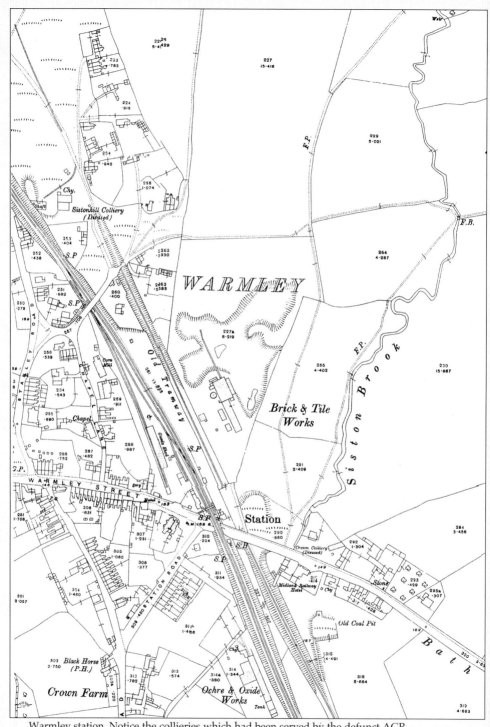

Warmley station. Notice the collieries which had been served by the defunct AGR.

Reproduced from the 25″, 1912 Ordnance Survey Map

A down view of Warmley *c.*1905 showing the 1899 timber footbridge. By 1912 its lattice work sides were boarded. All the station buildings were of timber. The level crossing gates are open for an up train which is signalled. A turn-out from the down line to the goods yard is in the foreground. Porter Victor Burge is nearest the camera and the signalman stands on his balcony. Notice a milk churn on one platform and a palm tree on the other.   *M.J. Tozer Collection*

Warmley seen from the cab of an Ivatt class '2' 2-6-2T on a Temple Meads to Green Park train in July 1963. The steel footbridge dates from 1929.   *W.F. Grainger*

Warmley view up 1948. The dark-coloured goods shed is on the passenger platform.
Author's Collection

Since closure, most of the line has become a Bath to Bristol walk and cycleway. The former shelter on Warmley down platform is used as a refreshment room, 23rd August, 1988. *Author*

For convenience the yard was usually shunted by up trains. As it was the opposite end of the station from the signal box, the points were operated from a ground frame. A train backed into the Long Road which could hold about 30 wagons, allowing it to be locked in the yard so as not to interfere with other traffic which wished to pass. The shunting neck was relatively short. When shunting was complete, the train drew forward on to the main line and if it was long, it meant that the engine almost reached Mangotsfield South Junction. The train then stopped so that the guard could close the ground frame. An alternative way of shunting was to leave the brake van on the main line, move forward and shunt wagons from the yard on to it. The afternoon 'Engine and Van' found the empties ready on the Outside Road having been prepared by the early morning shunt. One guard shunted very quickly much to the despair of a nervous porter, sometimes five rafts of wagons drifting down the gradient with but a small gap between each, the guard calling out the siding to the porter who was overwhelmed with the task of changing the points and trying to apply wagon brakes so that the wagons already standing in the sidings were not struck too hard and derailed.

Traffic consisted of general merchandise, while an adjacent brick and pipe works dispatched about three wagon loads of produce weekly. Cattle arrived about every three months. A special feature was the ochre traffic. The yard was red with it and when wet it coloured boots and socks, and when dry, blew about and made one's hair red. Black, blue, green and yellow ochre was also dealt with. Four to five wagons of ochre and about the same number containing coal arrived daily. The Back Road was kept for coal traffic while ochre traffic used the Outside Road as this had space for the ochre lorry to turn. In 1939 a lorry owned by Douglas motor cycles arrived every other day with a consignment of bikes from the factory at Kingswood. An LMS delivery lorry from St Philip's Goods Depot, Bristol arrived at about 9.30 am to collect parcels from the shed on the platform for delivery to Abson, Doynton, Mangotsfield, Pucklechurch, Shortwood and Wick. In earlier years an LMS dray delivered round Warmley. The weighing machine in the yard was worked by a railwayman from St Philip's. The crane was restricted to a maximum of 5 tons.

Latterly the station was supervised by the Bitton station master who arrived every Friday with pay, a Grade 1 porter working on each of the two turns, 3.30 am until 11.30 am and 11.30 am until the last train to Bath left at about 8.50 pm. A clerk came from Bitton about three times a week. The early turn porter unlocked the station and the late man closed it, each man having a set of keys. In 1939 the goods arrived at 3.45 am and as the passenger service had yet to start, the porter could give his entire attention to shunting. Warmley closed to goods on 17th May, 1965 and to coal traffic a few days later.

South of the level crossing over the A420 Bristol to Chippenham road the signal box remains, preserved as a listed building. During World War I coal was dug unofficially from the sides of cuttings between Warmley and Bitton, the holes being visible in the slopes for years afterwards.

The line descends at 1 in 204 to Oldland Common (127 miles 34 chains), opened 2nd December, 1935. Comprising sleeper-built platforms and simple waiting shelters, it was the only station on the line to be lighted by electricity.

The timber platform at Oldland Common station, view down on 16th February, 1967.   *Author*

The road level ticket office at Oldland Common after closure.   *W.F. Grainger*

The road level notice directing potential passengers, *c.*1966. *W.F. Grainger*

The site of Oldland Common Halt. *Reproduced from the 25", 1906 Ordnance Survey Map*

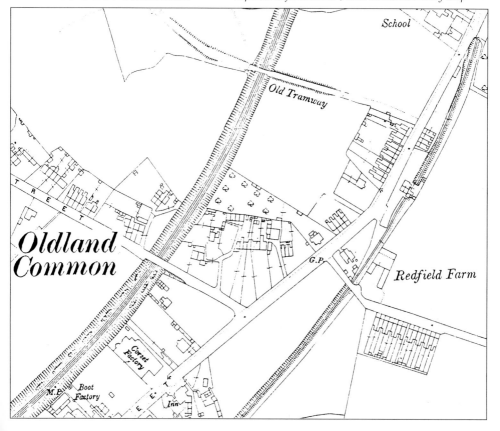

A 1908 view looking towards Willsbridge with Bitton station drive rising on the right.
Author's Collection

A class '1P' 0-4-4T approaches Bitton with an up stopping train, 12th April, 1906.
Author's Collection

Well used, trains picked up more passengers here than at Bitton. During the severe winter of 1962-3 the manpower situation was such that snow and ice could only be cleared from one end, so the guard went through each train warning passengers to alight from the rear coach. Oldland Common was in the charge of the Bitton station master and dealt with parcels and miscellaneous traffic, but had no goods facilities. It became unstaffed on 7th December, 1964.

South of the station the Midland crossed the Avon & Gloucestershire Railway which was in a tunnel. Hitherto of natural stone, it was brick lined for 90 ft by the MR to bear the weight of main line trains. The MR steepened to the 1½ mile-long Bitton Bank of 1 in 121 (compare Colonel Yolland's report). The MR claimed 6 ft of land outward from the snowell (the Gloucestershire term for the centre of a hedge) so that their men could maintain the hawthorn. Boundary markers were made from old rail. The line passed through the heavy Bitton cutting, part of which is pennant rock from which fine stone was obtained for buildings and bridges.

Bitton (128 miles 34 chains) has a local stone-built main building on the down platform, this now forming the headquarters of the Avon Valley Railway. In design there were two pavilions with elaborate fretted barge boarding, while in the recess between these sections was a pierced iron canopy support. The building was not symmetrical as it had an additional office at the north end. The up platform had a stone-built shelter, cruciform in plan, its barge boards echoing those of the main building opposite.

The goods yard on the down side had four roads:

The Dock Road
The Goods Shed Road serving the stone building
Nos. 1 and 2 Goods Roads

The shunting procedure was as follows: an up train backed into the Dock Road. The 'dead end' held 15 to 16 wagons enabling the engine to shunt clear of the main line, the Shed Road being worked first. Room was available for lorries to load or unload at Nos. 1 and 2 Roads used by coal merchants. If these were full, the Dock and Shed Roads could be utilised. Other traffic dealt with was material to and from a paper mill, machinery and steel sheet, hides, chemicals from a works at Keynsham and moulding sand from a quarry in Ryedown Lane which was dispatched to Sheffield in a sheeted open wagon, the consignor insisting that the truck be clean so that the load would not be contaminated. During World War II Hill, Leigh & Co. Ltd, timber merchants, stored their supplies opposite the signal box as being less susceptible to German air attack than its main depot at Avonmouth. The goods crane was capable of lifting a maximum load of 4 tons.

Two 'pads' (a coffin-shaped wicker basket with a lid) of daffodils were taken daily during the season to St Philip's passenger station, Bristol, where they were sold. Another nursery sent flowers and cucumbers by rail, a van on the 6.55 pm ex-Temple Meads being filled and taken to Bath and going out on the 10.15 Perishables to Derby. Mushrooms loaded on two-wheel sack trucks were put on the 5.45 pm ex-Bath, the trucks being sent back empty from Mangotsfield after enabling a speedy transfer to be made between trains at Mangotsfield. Another

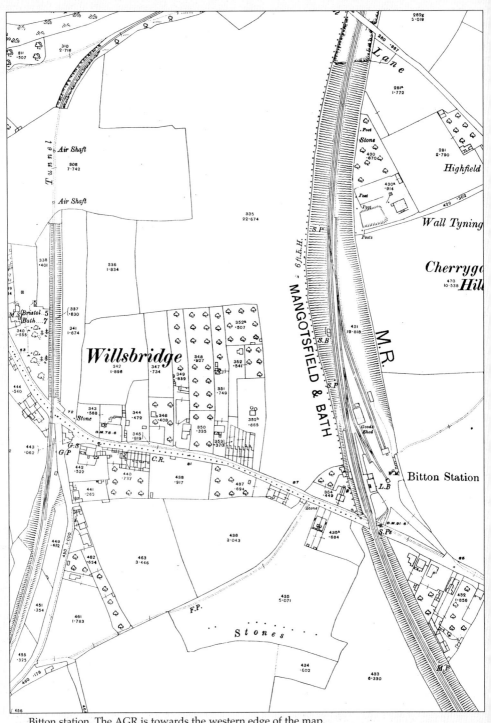

Bitton station. The AGR is towards the western edge of the map.
Reproduced from the 25", 1915 Ordnance Survey Map

'890' class 2-4-0 No. 89 entering Bitton was a down stopping train c.1910. A pigeon basket and milk churns are on the platform and a Norchard coal wagon from the Forest of Dean stands in the goods yard. *M.J. Tozer Collection*

Bitton station on 16th October, 1965, view towards Mangotsfield. Notice that the platform has been raised and both up and down roads relaid with flat-bottomed rail. *E. Wilmshurst*

The stone viaduct east of Bitton over the River Boyd, 19th April, 1980.   *Author*

The Avon Bridge, 19th April, 1980.   *Author*

Bitton nurseryman sent fruit to Glasgow and Edinburgh where they commanded a higher price.

At the turn of the century staff comprised the station master, porter, porter/signalman, junior porter, two signalmen, clerks and junior clerks, while in 1945 it was staffed by a station master with porter. There were but two signalmen, the box being closed at night. The Goods Shed Road was lifted in 1964 and the yard closed on 5th July, 1965.

Immediately south of the station the line crossed the A431 by a wrought-iron girder bridge and was carried on an embankment with a maximum height of 35 ft, nearly 1½ miles in length containing more than 400,000 cubic yds of material. The line crossed the River Boyd by a stone three-arch bridge with a height of 35 ft and span of 25 ft. Almost immediately afterwards, the Avon was crossed for the first time. The *Bath & Cheltenham Gazette* of 4th August, 1869 gave a comprehensive description:

> The bridge is a fine structure, made of wrought iron, lattice patterned, and built on the girder principle by Messrs Handyside & Co., of Derby, who are the manufacturers of all the wrought iron bridges on the line. It is supported by 10 cast iron pillars, screwed into the bed of the river, and consists of two spans, each 87 feet in width. It is from 40 to 45 feet above the water surface and is handsomely constructed and finished off with a pretty iron parapet and freestone pillars. On nearing Saltford the line cuts through the lias rock, and then runs along an embankment, leaving orchards burdened with fruit on the right, crosses the road of Saltford village and crosses the Avon a second time. The bridge is similar in construction to the other, the span being about 77 feet. In both of these bridges the railway runs on the tops of the girders, but in the remaining four it runs between them . . . A station for passenger traffic only is in the course of erection at Saltford, but it will not be opened for some time.

These two bridges, like all the others over the Avon, had their girder ends decorated with a scroll bearing a Wyvern.

Kelston (130 miles 60 chains) opened on 1st December, 1869, only three trains stopping each way daily and none on Sundays. Although earthworks allowed space for sidings to be laid, the option was never taken. The simple, stone-built offices were on the down platform, a timber shelter sufficing on the up. The station was ¾ mile over fields from Kelston and nearer Saltford just the other side of the river, a footpath alongside the railway giving easy access. Eager to win passengers from the GWR, the MR displayed a timetable board on the wall of the Bird-in-Hand Inn, Saltford. It is said that the local squire was allowed to have expresses stopped at Kelston, this being a condition under which the station was built. Kelston station was busy on the day of Saltford Regatta and also when a race meeting was held at Bath, passengers walking from the station to Lansdown 2½ miles distant, but involving a climb of 700 ft. The London & North Western Railway (LNWR) as well as MR ran race specials to Kelston and Bath. Almost half the passengers took the option of walking from Kelston instead of going into the city and obtaining transport. On these occasions there were plenty of railway police in evidence as bookies and punters tried to avoid paying their fares, while it was not unknown for bookmakers to run across the fields and hide in bushes by Kelston station and then leap into an up train. Race trains ceased to use Kelston after about 1930.

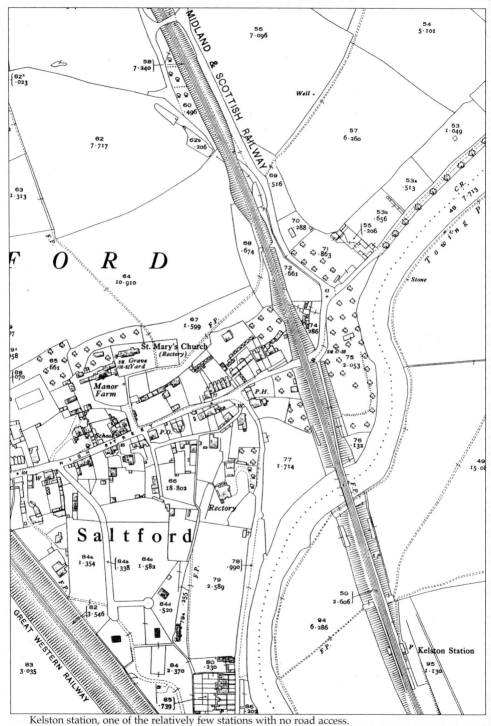

Kelston station, one of the relatively few stations with no road access.

Reproduced from the 25″, 1930 Ordnance Survey Map

Kelston station, which closed on 1st January, 1949, in a partly-demolished state on 22nd April, 1954. *Dr A.J.G. Dickens*

BR Standard class '5' 4-6-0 No. 73047 heads the down 'Pines Express' past an even more demolished Kelston station, 26th August, 1954. *Author*

At Newton Meadows class '4P' Compound 4-4-0 No. 41194 pilots class '2' 2-6-2T No. 41243 on the 9.05 am Temple Meads to Green Park, 28th August, 1954. No. 41194 was working to Bath to head an up express.   *Author*

Ex-GWR '28XX' class 2-8-0 No. 3804 at Newton Meadows with a down pigeon special *en route* to Templecombe on 8th August, 1959.   *Author*

Most passengers using Kelston station were anglers out for a day's fishing. Due to a reduction in the number of passengers using the station, the last train to stop was the 7.05 pm from Bristol on 31st December, 1948, after which the station's sole employee retired. The building on the down platform was not demolished until 1954. At one period it was staffed by a porter under the direction of the Weston station master, working a split shift, 6 am to 10 am and 6 pm to 10 pm, few trains calling during the middle part of the day. These times were highly inconvenient for a relief porter sent from Bath who had to make two trips daily. Once there the porter had an easy life, just looking after passengers, answering fishermen's queries regarding the last train and tending flower beds and lamps. Receipts were usually less than £1 per month, most tickets being returns issued elsewhere. One evening during World War II, a relief porter was on duty, and while the last train stood at the platform, a German plane dropped a flare which slowly descended and appeared to hang over the last coach. The terrified guard, expecting every moment to be bombed or machine-gunned, quickly waved the train off. This was a pity, because the porter intended catching it home and so had to walk to Bath. Kelston signal box only opened on summer Saturdays to shorten the block section from Bitton to Weston. At such times it was manned by either a relief signalman, or the 6 am-2 pm signalman normally at Weston who was relieved by his 2 pm-10 pm colleague; the latter arrived sufficiently early to enable him to travel to Kelston and remain there until traffic quietened.

Beside the Avon, the Midland paralleled the GWR line the other side of the river, occasional racing taking place on this stretch. It ran below Kelston Park and crossed a bridge into Newton Meadows, bisecting the huge Cavalry Field. After passing under the Bristol to Bath road and before crossing the Avon, in about 1950 a turnout was laid beside the up line ready to be put in to provide a private siding for Stothert & Pitt's storage ground. However the latter was never installed following a dispute over the securing of loads, Stothert & Pitt's not expecting that it would be necessary to secure a load so thoroughly for a journey of two miles as it would for one of two hundred. Consequently materials were moved by road to this ground.

The Midland crossed the Avon and entered Bath. At Avondale Road were two private sidings, the one to the west of this overbridge being for the Bath Brewery. The malthouse was built on land purchased from the MR. Opened on 10th November, 1896, the siding agreement was terminated on 31st March, 1968, the track being taken out of use on 5th May, 1968. Locomotives were not allowed into the sidings, but with a long train vehicles could be put in without the engine entering. With a short train, a rope was hooked to the wagons and a couple of turns made round an electrically driven (originally donkey-powered) capstan which drew the wagons in or out. The capstan was not always operational and the brewery staff often preferred to move vans with a pinch bar, this being a lighter task than moving the heavy wire rope.

Another method of shunting wagons in if a guard had a short train, was to cut the wagons off, shout to the two brewery employees standing by with brake sticks, 'They're all yours now' and shunt them into the siding smartly, the engine stopping before reaching the private track. Sometimes the men failed to

Locksbrook timber wharf siding *c.*1900, view west. The first private siding agreement was
signed on 15th December, 1871.   *Author's Collection*

The fire at Locksbrook timber wharf on 7th October, 1919. Firemen played water on the signal
post to prevent it igniting.   *Author's Collection*

halt them before they struck the blocks. Each box van contained 120 two hundredweight sacks of grain, making a total of 12 tons. If there was no traffic for the brewery, but empty vans were required to be removed, the guard made sure that there were 12 empty wagons behind the tender to reach the vans in the siding. This was normally shunted every day with 6 to 12 vans going in or out. The 'Pines Express' often passed while shunting was being carried out, so the guard had to be careful that he was not knocked down by it. Because of the sharp curve, the fireman generally had to get down and relay the guard's signal to the driver.

To the east of Avondale Road overbridge was a sharply curved siding to the clay mill and cement works of Messrs Shaw (agreement dated 15th December, 1871), later replaced by a short siding to Messrs J. Long's timber yard. Long's received batches of 30 wagon loads of timber imported at Avonmouth and Sharpness. As the siding was incapable of holding this number, any excess was put in Jobbins' coal siding at Weston station. When shunting Long's siding, a guard had to ensure that a runner wagon was always below overhanging timber. The siding was removed on 18th February, 1962. Locksbrook Wharf Timber Mill (later Long's) caught fire on 7th October, 1919 when a band saw overheated, igniting sawdust and shavings. As this conflagration was adjacent to the line, trains were held up, the 1.25 pm to Bristol St Philip's still standing at Weston station an hour later. Services re-started at 3 pm, first being soaked with water to prevent the coachwork paint blistering. The up advanced starter kept catching alight, its paint was burnt and a hose played on it to prevent its total destruction. The wooden boundary fence on the north side of the line smouldered and residents doused it with buckets of water, while jets were played on the sleepers to prevent them burning.

Weston (133 miles 67 chains) served the western outskirts of Bath and Twerton just across the river, although the village of Weston was a mile from the station. Until about 1948 the LMS maintained a billboard in the village High Street. The main building on the down platform was identical to that at Bitton, while the simple waiting shelter on the opposite platform was timber-framed. Latterly it was replaced by a red brick structure. As at Warmley, palm trees grew in the station garden. The down platform was 600 ft in length - twice that of the up, in order that it could be used as a ticket platform and also to start long excursion trains for the Somerset & Dorset Railway. During World War I hospital trains arrived with injured servicemen for the Bath War Hospital at Combe Park, on the site of the present Royal United Hospital. Tickets to the station were marked 'M&B' (Mangotsfield and Bath) to differentiate them from those to Weston-super-Mare. The station was renamed Weston (Bath) on 1st October, 1934.

The opening of Bath Electric Tramways on 2nd January, 1904 had a severe effect on passenger traffic (*see page 61*) as the trams offered a more frequent and cheaper service to the city, remaining rail passengers mostly travelling westwards.

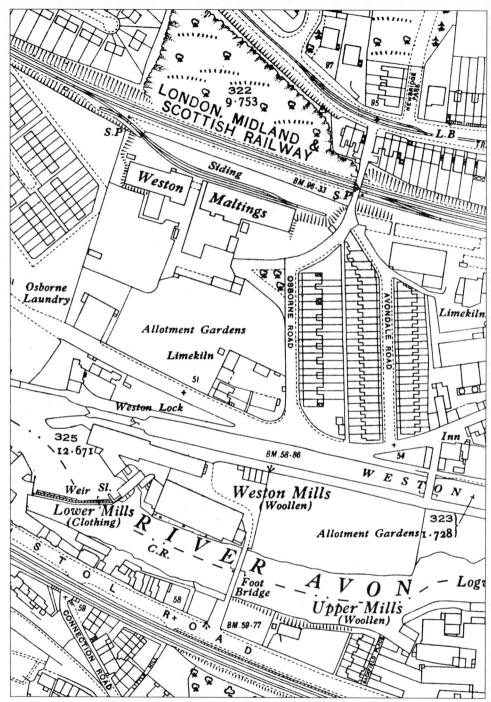

Weston brewery sidings. A passing loop on the Bath Electric Tramways route along Newbridge Road can be seen to the north. To the south lies the River Avon and the GWR line to Bristol.
Reproduced from the 25", 1932 Ordnance Survey Map

Weston station seen in the down direction from the signal box *c.*1905. The left-hand platform is longer than the up as it doubled as a ticket platform and had to be able to cope with a long express. Jobbins' coal yard and siding are on the right. The brewery ground frame's distant signal is below Weston's inner home.   *Author's Collection*

Class '2' 2-6-2T No. 41243 passes Weston signal box with an up stopping train.   *J. Hobbs*

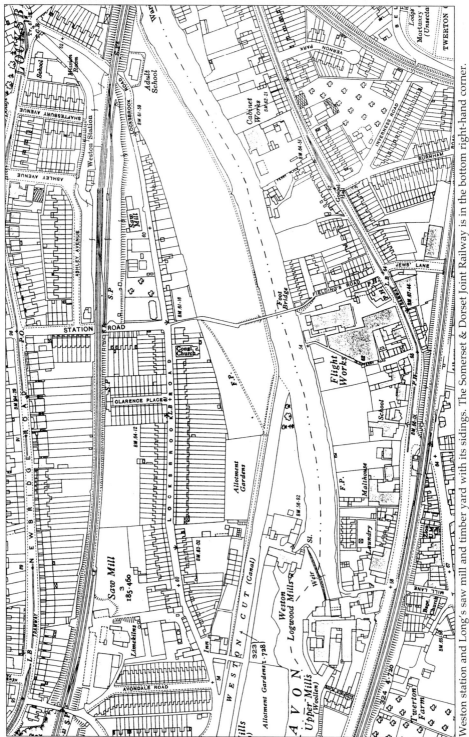

Weston station and Long's saw mill and timber yard with its sidings. The Somerset & Dorset Joint Railway is in the bottom right-hand corner. *Reproduced from the 25", 1930 Ordnance Survey Map*

Weston Station Statistics

Year	No. of season tickets	No. of passengers	Receipts £
1903	46	71,140	1,130
1904	35	21,801	753
1905	24	18,373	631

Just prior to closure on 21st September, 1953, only about a dozen people used Weston station daily. *Circa* 1945, staff consisted of a station master with a porter on each turn, the signal box being continuously manned.

The station had a siding, opened on 1st September, 1869, its principal traffic being coal; Charles Jobbins the station master for 27 years was also the coal merchant. The land is now a builder's yard. To avoid facing points, access to the yard, which was adjacent to the up line, was via a trailing point from the down line. As the yard was shunted by an up freight, it meant that the engine had to run-round the wagons before pushing them in. The turnout at the east end of the station could not be clearly seen from the signal box, and the guard pressed a plunger to indicate to the signalman by bell code:

1 bell - engine clear of crossover
2 bells - operate crossover from down main to siding
3 bells - engine out of siding

If the guard was co-operative he would help Miss Jobbins, who took over her father's business, by positioning a certain wagon at the correct bunker, for instance a Derby nuts wagon beside the Derby nuts bunker. If a guard merely left the wagons in the siding - all he was obliged to do - her men had to pinch bar them laboriously into position. The siding was shunted in the morning and also by the 2.10 pm pick-up goods. The siding also occasionally held locomotive coal for Bath if there was no room by the coal stage there.

It is interesting to record that Benjamin Colbourne, an MR goods guard newly arrived from Derby where he had seen a successful Co-operative Society, was encouraged by Jonathan Carr, owner of Twerton woollen mills, to found the Twerton Co-operative Society in 1888, its first shop being opened in February 1889.

East of the station the line crossed the Avon before Bath Junction signal box (134 miles 21 chains), where the S&D line joined for the final ½ mile to the terminus. The original MR signal box north of the line and the nearby S&D Bath Single Line Junction signal box both closed on 13th April, 1924, being replaced by a new box in the fork between the two lines. This box, in turn, closed on 12th September, 1966. West of the junction were the Bath Junction Yard sidings consisting of five roads.

Before a down goods from the Midlands arrived at the Junction Yard, the shunting engine was placed in the gas works siding out of the way. When the freight arrived it reversed into No. 1 Road which could hold almost 50 wagons. The engine uncoupled and proceeded to the motive power depot. The shunting engine was then brought from the gas works siding, coupled on and Roads 2 and 3 utilised to form trains for Templecombe and Bournemouth. No. 4 Road was for Bath Transfers such as timber for Hill's siding, coal for merchants and general merchandise for the shed and local traders. No. 5 Road held 'short

Weston down platform *c*.1905. Notice the flagpole at the far end of the building.
M.J. Tozer Collection

Weston view down 16th September, 1953. The brick shelter on the up platform had recently replaced a timber structure. Notice the gas lighting and that the lamp standards on the platforms are of a different pattern.   *Dr A.J.G. Dickens*

Class '4F' 0-6-0 No. 3876 passes Weston station 26th May, 1936. The concrete signal post was removed in the 1930s when upper quadrants were installed. The Brewery ground frame's distant is below Weston's inner home. The short pole for track circuit feed is to the right of No. 3876's smokebox. Charles Jobbins' Ford coal lorry can be seen on the right. To the left of the brake van is the original timber shelter on the down platform.   *Revd Alan Newman*

The bridge over Locksbrook Road, 27th January, 1979. When this bridge was renewed, the decorative cast-iron sides were retained.   *Author*

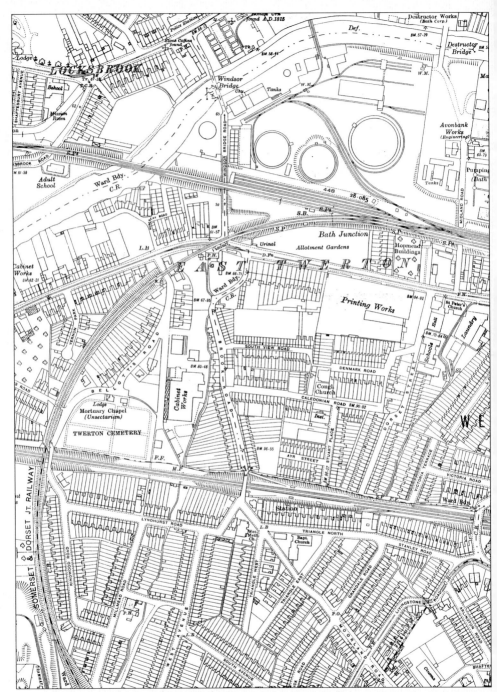

A map of Bath Junction and to the north the lines serving Bath gas works. The S&D line sweeping away to the south crosses the GWR main line just west of Oldfield Park station. The Destructor bridge, top, was the original Midland Railway bridge moved downstream to this site.
Reproduced from the 25", 1932 Ordnance Survey Map

traffic', in other words, wagons which were going only a few miles down the S&D and could be taken on the 5.50 am 'all stations to Templecombe', rather than be carried by a through train.

East of the Junction Yard were the sidings leading to Bath Gas Works and used for storing empty coal wagons. As well as serving the works on the south bank of the Avon, the line crossed the river by plate girder bridge to that on the north bank. At first probably horses drew wagons over the gas company's line, but in 1901 an Aveling & Porter geared locomotive was purchased new.

Bath Gas Works Engines

Loco. No.	Type	Builder	Works No.	Date	Remarks
-	0-4-0WT	Aveling & Porter	4909	1901	Purchased new, withdrawn June 1928
1	0-4-0ST	Peckett	1267	1912	Purchased new, scrapped about February 1964
2	0-4-0ST	Avonside	1978	1928	Purchased new, scrapped about February 1964
24	4wDM	Ruston & Hornsby	210479	1941	Purchased about February 1964 from Thos. W. Ward Ltd, Templeborough Works, Sheffield. Went to S&D Railway Circle, Radstock November 1971.
23	4wDM	Ruston & Hornsby	306089	1950	Purchased about February 1964 from Thos W. Ward, Templeborough Works, Sheffield. Went to Stapleton Rd Gas Works, Bristol June 1971.

The gas works was the principal user of the Mangotsfield to Bath line, about 40 wagons arriving daily, carrying about 3,200 tons of coal per week. When snow thawed and re-froze forming an ice block in a coal wagon it was almost impossible to extract the coal, Bath gas works had an unusual, if not unique, method of thawing it out by placing a tray of burning coke beneath the frozen wagon. Some coke left by rail. *Circa* 1964 a siding was laid at the works for naphtha rail tankers, but never used as this commodity always arrived by road.

At the west end of the Midland Bridge Road Goods Depot shunting spur stood BP petrol tankers being discharged, and when a driver was shunting a long train he had to beware of striking them. A shunting engine was placed against them when they were being unloaded and while it was waiting for a train to come in. Another hazard was that the tanks had to be fly-shunted in. South-east of Bath Junction was a siding added on 30th April, 1931 and worked by Hopmead ground frame. Here hopper wagons dropped coal for the Bath Co-operative Society. Hopmead Buildings was a row of houses built by the MR for its employees. Further east the S&D locomotive shed could be seen below the main line, the Boat Road running along the river bank behind the locomotive depot.

On 15th July, 1875 Samuel Robertson, a Bristol contractor, signed an agreement to erect a goods shed for transferring traffic between rail and river,

Right: Bath Gas Works locomotive No. 1, Peckett No. 1267 of 1912 on 21st March, 1959. Notice the beam to prevent it sinking too far when derailed.
Revd Alan Newman

Below: Bath Gas Works No. 2, Avonside No. 1978 of 1928, 21st March, 1959.
Revd Alan Newman

Below: Bath Gas Light & Coke Co. wagon No. 3, built by Gloucester Railway Carriage & Wagon Co., January 1905. Livery was principally a lead colour with black fittings and white lettering shaded black.
Author's Collection

its roof covering both rail wagons and barges. The MR operated a fleet of at least five boats, endeavouring to build up a useful feeder service. Two of the vessels were purchased from Robbins & Company, boatbuilders, Bradford-on-Avon. A depot was opened at Frome Road, Bradford-on-Avon, and stabling rented at the Barge Inn for £80 a year. Traffic was light, a maximum of 2½ tons of rags being taken to Bradford, return loads consisting of rubber or flock rarely exceeding a ton. The lightness of traffic caused the Midland to purchase three narrow boats in 1871, being more economical to operate than barges. The MR Trowbridge depot was at the Town Bridge, on the corner of Mill Lane, paper for the *Wiltshire Times* arriving by canal and being carried onwards to the publishers by MR steam lorry. The MR barge service ceased on 31st May, 1912. The only mishap recorded occurred in 1884 when the MR's barge *Jenny* fractured the chain of the crane at Dundas Wharf, causing the railway company to be fined £14 14s. 7d.

From the Boat Road a siding led into Stothert & Pitt's (S&P) Victoria Works; the private siding agreement was made on 15th January, 1898, Stothert's paying an annual rent of 10 per cent of its cost of £130. This firm was a principal crane builder. Wagons on S&P tracks were shifted by suitably adapted Fordson tractors. S&P products went to various places for export, much of it carried on long wagons, either bogie vehicles or long wheelbase four-wheelers, derailments sometimes occurring on the twisting road.

Special instructions were issued for working traffic to and from the steeply graded Riverside lines:

INSTRUCTIONS TO BE OBSERVED RESPECTING THE WORKING OF TRAFFIC TO AND FROM THE RIVERSIDE LINES

Movement must not be made to or from the Riverside Lines without the permission of the Shunter in charge.

Before permission is given by the Shunter in charge for a movement to be made to or from the Riverside Lines, a man appointed for the purpose must walk over the lines leading to and from the Riverside Lines.

This man, on ascertaining that the lines over which the movement is to be made are clear, must signal to the Shunter in charge.

He must then proceed at once to the vehicular level crossing to control the movement of road and rail traffic thereon.

Scotch blocks protecting the Riverside Lines are provided at the lower end of the Boat Road, and it is the responsibility of the Shunter in charge to obtain the key from the Foreman in charge of the Running and Maintenance Depot, and seeing the Scotch Blocks are again secured in the safety position on completion of shunting, returning the key to the Foreman in charge of Running and Maintenance Depot.

These instructions also apply to movements made to or from the Riverside Lines by the Running and Maintenance Staff when Operating Staff are not in Attendance.

The Midland Bridge Road Goods Depot at Bath between the main line and the Lower Bristol Road was quite extensive, being laid out with four sidings, then the Shed Road, the Stone Road, four coal roads, the Loading Dock Road, wagon repair road and Hill Leigh's timber siding. Through cattle trucks were held on the Stone Road, this being convenient for their removal. Brake vans were also kept on this road and, on one occasion, one man shunted four in,

MR narrow boat No. 3 on the Kennet & Avon canal at Dundas, east of Bath, *c.*1900.
Author's Collection

MR narrow boat at Dolemeads wharf, Bath *c.*1905 before ascending the staircase of locks.
Author's Collection

Stothert & Pitt's had a large engineering works whose principal manufacture was cranes. They had an internal railway system on which wagons were moved by Fordson tractors fitted with buffer planks. They also had a rail-mounted crane as depicted here in 1931. *Author's Collection*

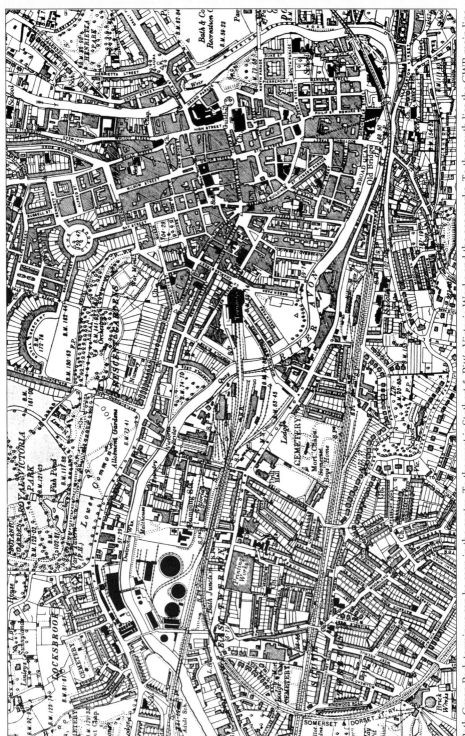

Bath Green Park terminus can be seen in the centre. To the west is Stothert & Pitt's Victoria Works and the gas works. To the south lies the GWR main line with Oldfield Park station *left*, and Bath station, *extreme right*.

Reproduced from the 6", 1930 Ordnance Survey Map

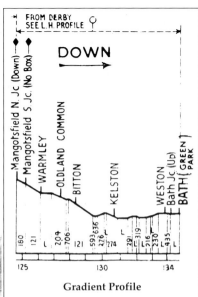

Gradient Profile

Left: Stothert & Pitt's rail-mounted crane on the Boat Road, 17th February, 1966.

Revd Alan Newman

Below: Ex-GWR '57XX' class 0-6-0PT No. 3758 minus its brass cabside number plate, in front of the water softener *c.*1964. To the left is one of Stothert & Pitt's cranes.

Author

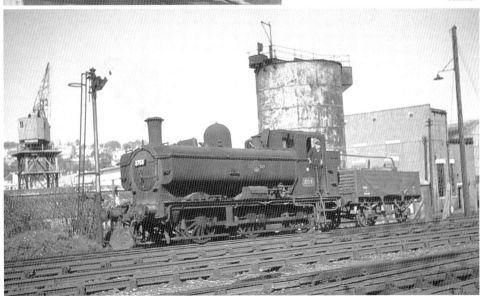

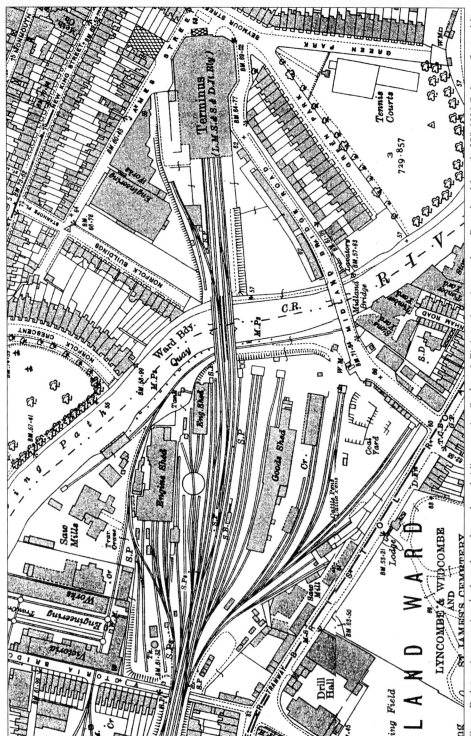

Green Park terminus, engine sheds and goods yards and sidings serving Stothert & Pitt's engineering works. *Reproduced from the 25″, 1936 Ordnance Survey Map*

yelling to a guard, 'They're all yours'. The road was so short that by the time the guard had climbed into one van and applied the brake, they had all gone through the stop blocks. Coal could only be unloaded from sidings 2 and 3, there being no road access to Nos. 1 and 4; these were used for empties and wagons awaiting unloading. Coal roads were shunted at about 4 pm. The 4 am goods to Gloucester took 50 empty wagons from the Dock Siding.

It was unusual for a local paper to report extensively on a goods station, but the *Bath Chronicle* did so on 10th March, 1870, as was recorded on page 19. Not content with this account, its edition of 28th April enthused:

The works which have been for a long time in progress in connection with the accommodation for the conduct of goods traffic for the Midland Railway, and which we noticed some two months since, are rapidly approaching completion; in fact, to all intents and purposes the work will be terminated on Monday next (2nd May) by the opening of the handsome new goods station in Sydenham Field. As regards the station itself, the arrangements, internally and externally, appear to be most perfect; the goods shed is admirably lighted and the effect of this combined with the colouring of the various parts of the building, is by no means inelegant. The apparatus is of an extensive nature, no less than eight substantial cranes being placed along the platform running down the centre of the shed, while four weighing machines are fixed at different points of the platform. Under this platform is a series of commodious cellars, which the Company intend to let for storage purposes, thus utilising them in the same way as those under the platform at the passenger station, which are leased by Mr R.B. Cater. [The 1870 *Bath Directory* stated that Cater was a grocer, wine and spirit merchant, and owned ale and porter stores.]

There are five entrances to the shed, consisting of massive doors sliding upon wheels. At the southern extremity of the building the offices are erected, separate rooms being provided for the manager and the clerks respectively, and these have been adequately fitted up with the requisite office appliances. The raised area surrounding the goods shed is traversed in several directions with sidings and lines of railway, and provision has been made in this respect for the retention of at least 40 wagons in the vicinity of the goods shed. The premises cover an area of about four acres, and the raised level on which stand the station and its surroundings has been covered with pitching of an enduring character, and well calculated to sustain the large traffic of which there is every prospect on the opening of the station.

(Between the road and railway bridges) . . . the company contemplate constructing a large steam crane, which will be used for the purpose of unloading stone, coal, and other goods from barges in the river below. [It is believed that this was never constructed.] In the other direction, at the side of the roadway leading from the Bristol-road, a ponderous weighing machine for carts and heavy purposes is fitted up, and further on, near the gate, there is a row of offices, (six in number), erected with the intention of being let by the Company to merchants and others.

Bath station was located at 134 miles 60 chains, the milepost (134¾) being sited at the buffer stops. Although *Bradshaw's Railway Guide* referred to the station as Queen Square, this was an unofficial appellation, locals always referring to it as the 'Midland Station'. The Green Park suffix was added on 18th June, 1951. In British Railways' days the branch was operated by the London Midland Region as a 'penetrating line' until 1st February, 1958, when it was transferred to the Western Region. Although several writers have stated that initially traffic was handled at a temporary station on the far side of the river, in fact the splendid

81   BATH. – Midland Railway Station.   L.L.

Bath Green Park exterior *c.*1905.   *Author's Collection*

Interior of the train shed *c.*1912.   *Author's Collection*

Concourse of Bath station *c.*1903. The buffers are on the right. *Author's Collection*

The concourse of Bath station *c.*1949. The stonework in the foreground was supplied by W. Mannings, a Bath builder, as an advertising feature. *Author's Collection*

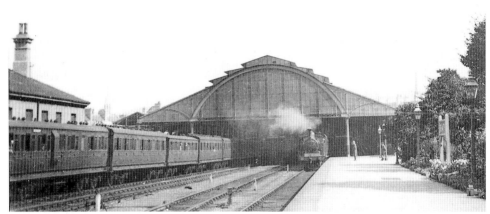

Bath, view towards the buffers *c.*1930. A class '1P' 0-4-4T is leaving for Bristol St Philip's. Notice the attractive garden on the right.   *Author's Collection*

A grounded MR Pullman coach at Bath in August 1935 by the end of the bonded store. Notice the nameboard on the seat back.   *J.E. Cull*

terminus was used from the outset, finishing touches being made while being used by passengers. The *Bath Chronicle* of 5th August, 1869 said:

> Much has yet to be done to render the station complete. At the entrance to the station there will be, when all is finished, a handsome pair of iron gates. Passing through the temporary wooden ones, on the left hand is a commodious cab stand, from which vehicles can approach the arrival platform to take up passengers and at once drive out by another road, while a railed off footbridge will be constructed for the convenience of pedestrians. [This was never built.]
>
> The station is a very handsome one, both platforms being 450 feet long and covered in for a distance of 220 feet. The roof, the central span of which is 66 feet, is painted in vermilion, chocolate and white. The painting is still being carried on by an ingenious moveable stage, constructed by Mr J. Green, the clerk of works; it is so managed that trains can pass in and out without interfering with it. On the arrival platform there is a commodious waiting room, neatly furnished, and attached to it is every convenience. The porters' room is next reached, and it is fitted in such a manner as to secure the comfort of the company's servants. The next apartments are a lamp room and are heated from below, in which footwarmers are intended to be kept. On the arrival platform a cloak room is provided and the apartments of the station master will be found here. The booking hall comes next, and we may here state that the entrance is covered, so that passengers may alight under shelter. The hall is a very spacious one, and the comfort of both the passengers and the booking clerk has been studied: when completed handsome settees will be supplied.
>
> That portion devoted to the clerks is covered with a light arched roof of diaper glass, an arrangement which will prevent the noise of the engines penetrating into that portion of the hall. There are two windows for the issue of tickets, and an arrangement for the safety of the money taken, is at once simple and effective. The money bowls are placed below each window, and covered by the counter, a portion of which slides back on pressing a spring, which is beyond the reach of anyone outside. Thus the booking clerk will be at liberty to attend to people at each window without any fears as to the safety of the cash under his charge, because he has only to draw forward the slide, which closes with a sharp click. The hall will be lighted by two large and elegant chandeliers. Having mentioned the arrival platform and its arrangements, we proceed to the departure side, which is reached without the aid of a bridge or crossing the line, as the platform is carried round one end of the station. There is a waiting room for second class passengers which is neatly furnished and lighted by brackets on the walls. A small room adjoining is to be fitted up as a restaurant in which dinners may be had. Connected with it are a cooking kitchen, and two bedrooms for the convenience of those connected with the refreshment department. The refreshment room is a large one, well suited to its purpose, and is fitted in a very elegant manner. The counter (in which are a spirit rail and two engines) has a marble top, and is a substantial affair. The best room in the building, we think - the ladies' first class waiting room - comes next, and is elegantly furnished. The chandelier is coloured blue, white and gold, and the chimney piece is of white marble. The gentlemen's first class waiting room is also a handsome apartment, and the chimney piece is also of marble painted with flowers. Attached to the room are a lavatory and closets. Under the platform are roomy cellars which will be let. A deal of work has yet to be done, but the amount of labour got through during Monday and Tuesday was surprising, as up to Monday afternoon there was no furniture in any of the rooms, and great credit is due to Mr J. Green for the energy in which he has displayed in forwarding the work. It should also be stated that the roof of the station, as well as the bridges spanning the river, have been erected under the skilful management of Mr Turnbull, from the works of Messrs Handyside, the contractors. We may mention that the side of the station which is open to Green Park will be covered with ornamental boarding.

Class '2' 2-6-2T No. 41240 ready to take a train to Temple Meads, 26th August, 1954.   *Author*

View from the cab of Ivatt class '2' 2-6-2T in July 1963 about to cross one of the parallel bridges over the Avon to collect SR coach set No. 966, on one of the middle roads. The squares at the end of the girder warn of limited clearance. Notice the water column and gas lamp to illuminate filling at night.   *W.F. Grainger*

It was certainly a superb building of outstanding merit, the pseudo-Georgian front block with its slender Ionic columns above the rusticated ground floor, balustraded parapet concealing the roof line and excellently proportioned fenestration, well balanced by a delicate iron *porte-cochère*, all complementing the train shed beyond.

By April 1870 the volume of passenger traffic rendered the accommodation so inadequate that the departure platform was extended 240 ft and the arrival side 120 ft to the river bridge. At the back of the latter platform a carriage dock was added.

The station remained largely unchanged until September 1931 when, instead of the booking office being in the central part of the hall, with first class passengers using the left-hand steps to their booking window, while third class passengers used the right-hand steps, the waiting room was partitioned down its centre to form new booking and parcels offices. The frontage of the station had to be slightly altered to give parcels access from the exterior to the new office. Apart from the economy of bringing parcel and booking offices under one chief clerk, the arrangement cleared the booking hall, letting passengers appreciate its full height, and gave a large, spacious circulation area.

Two large ticket racks were fitted either side of the booking window, the one on the left for singles and that on the right for returns. Additionally there was a small rack for such things as bicycle and pram tickets. At the end of each term, Kingswood, Monkton Combe and the Royal School sent down lists of pupils' ticket requirements, a clerk making them up in quiet moments, schools paying by cheque and collecting them. The booking clerks preferred dealing with Monkton Combe best as it informed pupils that their ticket order could not be altered. One school always seemed to ring up with cancellations, different destinations, or for a Circular Tour ticket to replace an ordinary one.

If a commercial traveller received a lift he sought a refund on the unused return half of his ticket and was given a rebate minus about five shillings. As the ticket was paid for by his firm, this was money in his pocket. Booking clerks were required to make a full balance each Saturday and had to remain on duty until 11 pm. On other days the office closed to the public about 7.30 pm, but on Saturdays was re-opened for the S&D 10 pm departure - a nuisance to the clerks as an interruption during totalling was annoying. On other days porters issued excess notes for the 10 pm train, the office supplying a bag with a pound float. In the 1950s £500 was taken in bookings for the 'Pines Express' on a Saturday, while weekly receipts at the station totalled some £6,000 to £8,000. Every morning cash was placed in a locked leather pouch, put in a locked box in a guard's van and taken to Bristol. Periodically the auditors arrived unannounced at Bath and took about half an hour to check tickets and cash. A Post Office telephone in the booking office was used to send telegrams. Booking clerks paid wages on Fridays in company with the station master's clerk who arrived with the cash.

The platform on the north side, originally the arrival side for Midland trains, held eight bogie coaches and locomotive, the south, originally departure side, held nine bogies plus engine. The arrival side had a carriage approach so that passengers could step from train to road vehicle, whereas on the departure side, they would have entered via the booking hall. For many years prior to closure the platforms were interchangeable, long trains tending to use the south

Right: The train indicator board in the booking hall. The white notice towards the bottom reads: 'Out of order'.
C. Steane

Far right: The ticket windows in the booking hall *c.*1965.
C. Steane

platform. Platforms were short for an important station, and coaches in excess of nine were on the river bridge. This caused confusion as passengers wishing to alight from the rear had to struggle along coach corridors to reach the platform, meeting others pushing in the opposite direction hoping to find vacated seats. The cost of extending the station over the river would have been prohibitive. To avoid passengers for Bath being overcarried, the guard was required to go through rear vehicles (which would have been off the end of the platform) before arrival and ask passengers to proceed along the corridor.

On the down 'Pines Express', Bath traffic was put in the front coaches as the rearmost were beyond the platform. One day an invalid for Bath was found in the last coach. The large windows of some of the coaches could be opened with a carriage key in order to facilitate loading or unloading of a stretcher. Donald Beale, the famous S&D driver, with his height was able to take the stretcher out through the window, a difficult procedure when not at a platform.

LMS guards working passenger trains destined for the S&D were required on arrival at Bath to hand over to the guard working forward the numbers and description of the vehicles and the tonnage of the train. S&D guards were given similar instructions. Points to release an engine from the northern platform were worked from a ground frame. The Departure Line ground frame gave access to and from the South centre road, while the Carriage Siding ground frame gave access to the carriage dock and bonded store. Parcels vans put on the dock road were taken out on the 10.15 pm Perishables to Derby. There was no water crane on the platform - unnecessary because engines were changed at Bath and tanks could be filled at the shed. A column on the west side of the bridge was used mainly by tank engines before returning to Bristol.

At the western end of the arrival platform the bonded warehouse (opened in April 1872) enabled vehicles containing wines and spirits consigned to various local traders to be shunted into a secure building, where they could be lowered by 3 ton crane to the cellars extending the full length of the station platforms, the casks being carried on small narrow gauge wagons. The liquor remained in store until its release from bond on payment of duty. The station gas pipes ran through the bonded stores and, in the event of a gas fault, permission had to be sought for fitters to enter. The bonded warehouse closed in January 1967.

In 1870 the *Bath Chronicle* reported that the untidy space between the station platform and buffers had been filled with earth in which evergreens and flowers were planted together with ornamental rock. This area was further improved in 1938 when builder W. Mannings maintained an ornamental garden free as an advertisement.

The S&D use of the station began on 20th June, 1874 putting Bath on a through route. The principal offices of the S&D were transferred in 1877 from Glastonbury to No. 14 Green Park Buildings and in 1902 extended into No. 13. As an economy measure they were moved into the station in 1930. From 1st June, 1930 Fishponds Control Office ceased to oversee the Bath branch, Bath Control Office opening on this date and taking over this duty and also the S&D lines.

There was a W.H. Smith & Sons' news stand on the platform until *c*.1951, and at one time a man travelled on the first train to Mangotsfield with a bag of papers to be sold from a stand there.

Bonded stores at the end of the arrival platform, 20th December, 1967.   *Author*

The Midland Railway stables at Bath on 25th June, 1966. The Midland Bridge can be seen in the background.   *Author*

Coaches and restaurant cars were gassed at Bath, the fuel arriving in tanks on an old LNWR coach underframe. It was recharged at St Philip's carriage sidings oil gas plant, travelling to Bristol every Monday on the 12.17 pm passenger from Bath. Gas lit coaches ceased before World War II, but restaurant cars were always topped up with gas. At Bath two Midland carriage and wagon examiners checked all S&D rolling stock about to go over the MR while two S&D men checked all Midland stock before it travelled over the S&D.

Following track lifting in 1967, after closure, the station became a temporary Christmas car park and was listed in November 1971 as a Grade 2 building. The City Council purchased the station and explored various uses such as an hotel, coach station, magistrates' court and concert hall, the final decision being that J. Sainsbury Ltd would build a supermarket on an adjacent site, renovating the station buildings. This was done very sensitively, and since the opening of the supermarket by Princess Margaret on 1st December, 1982, various rooms in the station have been taken over by small shops, while the train shed is used for open air events needing cover.

The last horse cab used the station on 7th January, 1914 when Charles Woods relinquished his sole right to ply cabs for hire at the terminus, a right he had held for 38 years. Bath Council's water supply tended to be badly depleted during times of light rainfall. On 17th March, 1934, during such a period, the *Bath Chronicle* reported:

Taxi drivers were busily washing their cars this morning when an old gentleman came along and strongly criticised their waste of water, reminding them of the dire penalties to which they were liable. It transpired that the taxis were not using 'company's' water at all, but were getting it from the railway's own non-drinking supply from Midford [*sic*-Devonshire] tunnel.

In 1870 stables were erected behind the departure platform, 10 horses occupying stalls in 1940; seven of these were used on goods, one on passenger-parcels work and two were kept spare. A horse keeper's cottage was located adjacent to the stable yard. The carts were left on the approach road to the arrival platform, the horses making their own way round the front of the station to their stables. Horses were not entirely replaced by mechanical transport until September 1951, though as early as 1904 one Thornycroft and a Straker steam wagon were in use, while three Mann steam wagons appeared two years later. In the late 1930s a Raleigh three-wheel van, a four-wheel Jowett and a horse van were all in use. In British Railways' (BR) times a parcel lorry left the station twice daily with a good load, the Western Region also sending a vehicle over to deliver to certain areas. Stothert & Pitt's brought articles to the station for the 'Pines Express' to take to Liverpool. Sometimes these weighed 2 to 3 cwt and if so, the firm's men remained to assist porters lift the parts into the van. Blooms were dispatched to Manchester about twice a week, practically the whole year round, while just prior to Christmas there were so many that they were loaded into a van and coupled behind the engine so that when the 'Pines' arrived, the engine and van both backed on. A barrow load of Bayer's brassières went out every night with the up Perishables. Sometimes Harris of Calne had a rush order to fulfil, and it was brought to Bath by road where it was placed on rail.

At times during World War II Bath goods yard became highly congested, for a train of Army tanks took up an entire siding. In order to ease the siding situation, at weekends 50 empty coal wagons were stabled in one of the platform roads and left for Gloucester at 4 am each Monday.

The refreshment room was not only used by passengers, but by people coming in from outside to make use of its facilities. Luncheon baskets containing ham salad and bread rolls were prepared for the up 'Pines' and hampers of dirty cups came to be washed. On Saturdays, junior catering assistants had a tea urn and ice cream to sell from a trolley which was pushed up and down the platform. Refreshment room staff had bedroom accommodation upstairs; c.1935 three to four ladies were employed in the refreshment room. Takings were added to the booking clerks' receipts.

Between 8 and 8.30 pm on Saturdays pigeon clubs set up tables at Bath, fanciers counting the birds and loading the baskets on long barrows which were placed in vans and taken to Mangotsfield and made up with similar vans from Bristol into a train for the North. Porters disliked handling pigeon baskets because of the smell and mess of their occupants. Incoming pigeons were released from Bath Goods Yard which was open with no overhead wires.

The station master originally had living accommodation in the north-east corner of the station, but in later day these rooms were taken over as office accommodation for MR and S&D staff. On the north-west end of the building and set back from the platform was the fish store, its roof still sporting an enormous ventilator. It was later converted into a guards' room. A public address system was installed on the platforms about 1954, first as a temporary measure for summer use and then as a permanent feature. About five minutes before a train arrived, wooden barriers were pulled across the platform and porters collected passengers' tickets. The MR had a parcel and ticket office in the centre of Bath at 24 New Bond Street. In 1934 it was closed as an economy measure.

The station let its hair down on 9th June, 1961 when it was used as the venue for the 'Eleven O'clock Special', an event organised by the Bath Festival. Dancing took place on the platform, the film *The Titfield Thunderbolt* was shown in the waiting room, and a diesel multiple unit (dmu) shuttle ran to a barbecue at Wellow. Four years later, Green Park as a typical 19th century terminus was used for filming scenes from R.L. Stevenson's comedy *The Wrong Box*.

This scene shows 3,300 pigeons being released at Bath LMS goods depot in May 1934. The grain shed is on the right. The 'N' on the carriage truck in the lower right-hand corner, stands for 'Not Common User'.   *Author's Collection*

Chapter Six

Closure

The line was listed for passenger service withdrawal in the 1963 Beeching Report, the freight side being more healthy. The relatively low passenger receipts were in part due to passengers from the North of England being actively diverted from the Somerset & Dorset line, being booked via alternative routes; these being longer, cost the travelling public more money. This was to 'prove' that the S&D route carried insufficient traffic. The proposal to withdraw the passenger service was announced in June 1965 to take effect that September, but postponed because objections were received which needed to be considered by the Transport Users' Consultative Committee. Eventually the line closed to passengers on 7th March, 1966 (the same day as the S&D shut), goods trains continuing to run. The 29th January, 1967 saw the track from Mangotsfield station to Mangotsfield South Junction closed and the track lifted east of 134 miles 34 chains. Green Park station became a temporary car park to accommodate Christmas shoppers, later that year. On 5th May, 1968 the branch was singled and designated a siding from Mangotsfield North Junction to Bath, with a speed limit of 40 mph. The down line was used as far as Kelston Woods where a landslip, or threatened slip, made it more sensible to use the former up road. Double track remained east of Weston level crossing. When the line from Lawrence Hill Junction, Bristol, to Yate was closed to passengers on 3rd January, 1970 and trains diverted via the former GWR route, Bath trains used the former up line north of Mangotsfield, the down main being retained for Plasser track machine driver training.

Bath gas works continued to receive 3,200 tons of coal weekly but with the introduction of North Sea gas and the consequent closure of Bath gas works in May 1971, the branch closed on 28th May, 1971. After this date, condemned vans were stored in the yard awaiting breaking up, the author seeing an up train of about 40 vans leaving Bath in mid-April 1972. Lifting commenced on 8th May, 1972, Eagre (Scunthorpe) Ltd using class '08' diesel locomotive No. 3517, bogie bolster and contractor's crane to raise rails and sleepers together, some of this track being relaid on the former Thornbury branch to serve the Tytherington quarries which were being developed. This branch had closed on 30th September, 1967 and the track lifted. For more details see *The Yate to Thornbury Branch*, by Colin G. Maggs, published by The Oakwood Press.

The Bristol Suburban Railway Society, now the Avon Valley Railway, reopened Bitton station in 1972, laid a length of track and has gradually extended its line to reach Oldland Common. The restored goods shed at Bitton is used as a workshop.

The railway formation from Rudmore Park to Mangotsfield was turned into a walkway and cycle track in 1979. It was extended from Mangotsfield down the former Gloucester to Bristol line as far as St Philip's. Finished in 1986, the 20 km-long Bristol and Bath Railway Path for pedestrians, cyclists and wheelchair users, was the first major project of its kind in Britain. A special feature is a

'Peak' class diesel-electric No. D116 with a train to Temple Meads on 28th April, 1962.

R.E. Toop

Swindon 3-car 'Cross-Country' dmu working a Gloucestershire Railway Society special. Notice the station loudspeaker in the top right-hand corner.   *Lens of Sutton*

BR Standard class '5' 4-6-0 No. 73050 arriving at Bath with a train from Bournemouth West
c.1963.   *Dr Christopher Kent*

Cab view from an Ivatt class '2' 2-6-2T working a Temple Meads to Green Park train standing at
the down end of the Bath platform at Mangotsfield.   *W.F. Grainger*

A BR Standard class '5' 4-6-0 stands on the only remaining lattice bridge after the 1930s - that just west of Green Park station.   *Dr Christopher Kent*

'Castle' class 4-6-0 No. 7023 *Penrice Castle* passing Bath Junction with a Home Counties Railway Society special on 7th June, 1964.   *Author*

'Peak' class diesel-electric No. D43 passes Newton Meadows with a down goods, 14th June, 1968. The track has been singled, but the former down line not yet lifted.   *Author*

series of sponsored sculptures at points of interest. Most are dual purpose serving as seats or drinking fountains as well as being works of art. In 1979 its site was suggested as suitable for one of the projected Avon Metro lines, a link being proposed west of Bath to join British Rail before the proposed Twerton station, the Metro's terminus being Bath Spa. By 2005 this plan was moribund due to lack of financial support.

Probably the last passenger train to visit Bath before track lifting was the 'Somerset Rambler' in November 1970. The 3-car Gloucester Railway Carriage & Wagon Co. 'Cross-Country' set headed by No. 51063 stands at the entrance to the coal yard.

R.J. Cannon/Author's Collection

Left: Driver Sam Randle and '1347' class 2-4-0 No. 198, shed plate 3, Saltley, at Bath, 11th August, 1928. This locomotive was withdrawn in December 1930.
Colin Roberts Collection

Below: '1282' class 2-4-0 No. 157 and '890' class 2-4-0 No. 92 at Bath, 27th May, 1933. No. 92 is being prepared for a train which departed at 2.00 pm for a non-stop run to Mangotsfield where the coaches were attached to an express from Bristol to the North.
Revd Alan Newman

Chapter Seven

Locomotives

For many years, until the late 1940s, Bath to Bristol stopping passenger trains were handled very efficiently by Johnson class '1P' 0-4-4Ts, Nos. 1274-81 being sent to Bristol in 1875 for use on local services to Bath etc. Although this class was generally well-liked, large drivers found their cabs a little too cramped for comfort. Tank engines normally worked chimney first to Bristol. Expresses were handled by 2-4-0s and 4-4-0s, single-drivers appearing in earlier days. Goods trains were worked by 0-6-0s of various classes.

At one time Somerset & Dorset engines in their blue livery made regular trips over the MR between Bath and Gloucester, with occasional trips to Birmingham. In November 1933 ex-S&D 4-4-0 No. 44, numbered 633 in LMS stock, was fitted with a Dabeg feedwater heater and pump and worked on the 'Pines Express'. The Dabeg company claimed that the apparatus reduced fuel and water consumption, saved boiler maintenance and allowed longer periods between washouts, but the LMS found savings were insufficient to cover its cost of £425, though No. 633 retained the Dabeg heater until the locomotive was withdrawn in November 1959. When No. 633 was at Bath it also had patent firebars.

Due to weight restrictions, the S&D 2-8-0s had to be shedded at Radstock initially until the work of renewing the two underbridges between Bath Junction and the locomotive depot, started in 1914, was complete, the Butterley Company supplying the metalwork. Towards the end of 1935 a London, Tilbury & Southend section Whitelegg class '2P' 4-4-2T No. 2103 was tried on stopping trains to Bristol and though it rode very well and was marginally more powerful than a class '1P' 0-4-4T, it proved very heavy on coal and primed badly. With the near-completion of the bridge rebuilding programme in 1937, Compounds and 'Black Fives' were allowed over the line, subject to a speed restriction over Kelston bridge which still awaited reconstruction. This helped to ease overcrowding on summer Saturdays at Bath shed as it meant that one engine could haul a train from the Midlands, whereas hitherto two class '2P' 4-4-0s had usually been required.

No. 5440 was the first 'Black Five' to arrive and stayed until the 1950s. Following completion of bridge renewal, only 'Royal Scots' in their original condition and larger locomotives were prohibited. Class '8F' 2-8-0s appeared, with 'Crabs', 'Patriots' and 'Jubilees' less frequently. Standard class '5' Nos. 73050-2 arrived in 1954, the last Stanier 'Black Fives' leaving in 1958.

Stanier class '3P' 2-6-2Ts were allocated to Bath in 1938, those involved being Nos. 115, 179,180/1. This class was unpopular, most drivers claiming that they quickly lost steam. Of the two engines at Bath, one, usually No. 115, was used on stopping passengers to Bristol, while the other, often No. 181, shunted Bath Junction Yard and banked S&D trains to Combe Down tunnel.

During World War II the largest passenger engines normally on the line were 'Black Fives', though soon after the outbreak they were temporarily removed.

Class '1P' 0-4-4T No. 1339 on a train to Bristol St Philip's, standing by the bonded store.
Author's Collection

Class '1P' 0-4-4T No. 1331 at Bath *c*.1910.   *Author's Collection*

Three coal-rail class '1P' 0-4-4T No. 1251 outside the bonded store, 16th July, 1936.
Revd Alan Newman

Class '1P' 0-4-4T No. 1397 *c.*1938. *Author's Collection*

Class '2P' 4-4-2T No. 2103 (formerly London, Tilbury & Southend Railway No. 62 *Camden Road*) beside the water softener on 10th October, 1935. Class '1P' 2-4-0 No. 20092 on the left was transferred away from Bath soon after this picture was taken. No. 2103 was also at Bath from 16th July, 1936 to 22nd August, 1936. *J.E. Cull Collection*

Class '2P' 4-4-2T No. 2103 at Bath with a train to Mangotsfield on 16th July, 1936. A grounded MR Pullman car is in the background. *Revd Alan Newman*

Class '1P' 0-4-4T No. 1406 passing Newton Meadows with the 11.30 am St Philip's to Bath on 25th September, 1948. (This was the first railway photograph your author took.)   *Author*

Class '3P' 2-6-2T No. 181 standing by the water softener *c.*1940.   *Author's Collection*

Class '3P' 4-4-0 No. 715 at Bath in July 1938.   *Revd Alan Newman*

Class '2P' 0-4-4T No. 1900 on one of the centre carriage roads at Bath *c*.1947. Its previous shed had been 20E Manningham. The class was built new by Stanier with second-hand boilers from Johnson '1P' class 2-4-0s and rebuilt Kirtley class '2F' 0-6-0s.   *M.E.J. Deane Collection*

Compound No. 1046, one of the replacement engines, was even found to work satisfactorily over the steeply-graded S&D line. In November 1941 Drummond 'Small Hopper' 'K10' class 4-4-0s Nos. 135, 388/9 were on loan to the LMS from the Southern Railway, and shedded at Bristol. Classified '2P', these mixed traffic engines included goods trains to Bath in their duties. Nos. 388/9 remained at Bristol until March 1945. Drummond 'S11' 4-4-0 Nos. 395-404, lent to the S&D during World War II, occasionally appeared on passenger or freight duties on the Mangotsfield line and when working an up goods tended to slip to a halt at Mangotsfield South Junction. Southern 'West Country' and 'Battle of Britain' engines have run light over the line to turn at Mangotsfield when the Bath turntable has been under repair. *Circa* 1943, WD No. 179, formerly GWR 'Dean Goods' No. 2466 ran light over the line *en route* from the north to Blandford Camp, while *c.*1944 WD 2-10-0 No. 73777 hauled a down goods, returning the next evening on the 9.15 pm to Water Orton. Turning at Bath, it knocked off about 10 handles on SR coaches standing on an adjacent siding. Subsequently a notice appeared warning crews take care when turning 2-10-0s. An ex-LNWR 'Super D' 0-8-0 was seen on an up freight on 11th September, 1946, while another, No. 48927 from Bletchley, arrived on 15th January, 1956.

In March 1947 several class '4F' 0-6-0s appeared temporarily on stopping trains instead of the usual tank engines. Although oil-burning locomotives worked over the S&D in October 1947, among them class '5' No. 4830, the author did not see one on the Mangotsfield line until 28th February, 1948. From January 1947 most of the Johnson class '1P' 0-4-4Ts were replaced by Stanier class '2Ps' of the same wheel arrangement, Nos. 1900/2/3/4. These engines were run down and very poor steamers, but after repairs were greatly improved. As the water tank projected back into the cab it could be utilised as a seat by the fireman. As it felt cold to the posterior, one fireman insulated himself using his coat. It blew away in Newton Meadows and was later recovered from the Avon. His name was inside and he was contacted to make sure that he had not drowned.

The '2P' 0-4-4Ts did not stay long, being replaced in October 1949 by Ivatt class '2' 2-6-2Ts Nos. 41240-3, new, ex-works and quickly becoming great favourites with crews being comfortable, speedy and free steaming. Ivatt class '4MT' 2-6-0 No. 43012 was first seen by the author on 9th July, 1948, while in May 1951 both class '2' and class '4' 2-6-0s appeared quite frequently on freight working. In August 1948 Fowler class '3P' 2-6-2T No. 29 made a temporary appearance, and an ex-WD 2-8-0 was seen on 29th April, 1950. Class '1P' No. 1406 worked stopping passenger trains in August 1950, the first 0-4-4T to be used for many months, while the last 0-4-4T engine seen was No. 58072 (ex-LMS No. 1379) in May 1955. Ivatt 2-6-2T No. 41240 was transferred to Bristol (Barrow Road) in September 1953. In August 1955 many goods trains were hauled by 4-6-0s, both LMS and BR Standard class '5s', instead of 0-6-0s or S&D 2-8-0s. For the 1955 summer timetable, the 7.01 am stopping passenger from Bath Green Park to Bristol Temple Meads was hauled by a 4-6-0, usually a BR Standard class '5', instead of the usual tank engine. That August, Fowler class '4' 2-6-4T No. 42338 appeared on several permanent way trains, this class being hitherto, and subsequently, unknown on the line. On 11th June, 1955 ex-WD 2-8-0

Large-boilered class '7F' 2-8-0 No. 13806 (22C, Bath) on the Boat Road *c.*1937.
Colin Roberts Collection

Class '7F' 2-8-0 No. 53801 (71G, Bath) and a relatively rare visitor, class '5' 2-6-0 No. 42939, pictured at Bath on 11th May, 1957. *Revd Alan Newman*

No. 90340 from Mexborough and, on 12th January, 1956, No. 90149 from Gloucester were spotted; on 31st July, 1956 BR Standard 2-10-0 No. 92049 from Toton shed left on the 9.15 pm up freight. In the summer of 1958 BR Standard '3MT' 2-6-2T No. 82037 arrived at Bath, while the following year, Nos. 82004/41 were allocated to Bath, No. 41241 being transferred to Wellington. The class '3s' took over virtually all of the Bath turns, Nos. 41242/3 then seeing very little service over the line. On 30th August a BR Standard class '9' 2-10-0 hauled an up Saturday passenger train, the first time the author had seen this class on the line, while on 23rd February, 1960 No. 92113 worked the 10.15 pm Perishables just prior to trials of this class over the S&D the following month. Rebuilt 'Royal Scots' put in an occasional appearance, for example No. 46100 *Royal Scot* on 10th June, 1961 with the down Leicester Parcels, returning on the up 'Pines'; No. 46157 *The Royal Artilleryman* on 23rd July, 1961 and No. 46103 *Royal Scots Fusilier* on 25th February, 1962. 'Britannia' class Pacifics were rare, but No. 70014 *Iron Duke* and No. 70034 *Thomas Hardy* have been recorded. On 11th June, 1965 BR Standard class '4' 2-6-4T No. 80064 appeared on a Bath to Bristol stopping passenger train. Engines of this class had worked over the S&D for more than a year previously but had not been seen on the Mangotsfield line before.

After ex-GWR twin diesel railcars made a gauging trip over the line on 19th February, 1953, railcars, both single, twin, or two singles coupled, made one trip daily over the line starting with the winter timetable on 21st September, 1953. With single railcar working, a trailer was rare. Occasionally a railcar was replaced by a '45XX' 2-6-2T or an 0-6-0PT hauling a two-coach set. In February 1959 a 3-car BR dmu worked the 5.43 pm Bath Green Park to Bristol Temple Meads, a very rare occurrence. Following the amendment of BR's Regional boundaries in February 1958 when the Western Region gained full control of Green Park, 'Jinties' were replaced on shunting duties by WR 'Pannier' tanks, No. 3742 being recorded in January 1960. In 1958 No. 5934 *Kneller Hall* appeared on a pigeon special and on 18th February, 1959 a Collett '22XX' 0-6-0 was noted on a permanent way train; 2-6-0 No. 5393 made several trips Bath to Westerleigh in April 1959 and 2-8-0 No. 3804 arrived with a down pigeon train on 8th August, 1959. On 1st August, 1964 No. 4992 *Crosby Hall* worked the 2.10 pm pick-up goods, its crew only being allowed 45 minutes preparation time - the same as for a '4F' - whereas WR men would have been given longer for such an engine. On 19th August, 1962 an up train of 15 bogie vans was 'Castle'-hauled. Rare visitors indeed were Eastern Region 'B1' class Nos. 61152 and 61027 in May 1960, and No. 61143 on 28th July, 1965. In November 1965 a '51XX' or '61XX' 2-6-2T appeared several mornings on the 7.15 to Temple Meads, normally an Ivatt class '2' working. On 12th February, 1964 the author saw a 'Western' class diesel-hydraulic on the line for the first time. It was hauling the 5.10 pm Temple Meads to Green Park.

Most of the top link drivers at Bath were trained to operate diesels at the end of 1960 as they were to be used on the 'Pines Express' and some goods trains. From 11th September, 1961, the first day of the winter timetable, the 'Pines' was regularly hauled by a 'Peak' class diesel-electric, while a member of the same class was sometimes to be seen hauling a stopping train of two or three coaches, the 10.10 am ex-Green Park being one such example. Brush type '4' (now class

Class '3P' 2-6-2T No. 40174 passing Newton Meadows with the 11.35 am Bristol St Philip's to Bath and Bournemouth West, 9th April, 1949. It wears an early BR livery.   *Author*

'Jubilee' class '6' 4-6-0 No. 45594 *Bhopal* near the turntable, July 1961.   *Revd Alan Newman*

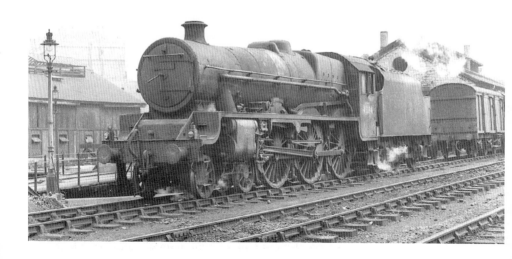

BR Standard class '9' 2-10-0 No. 92204 beside the breakdown train's tool van, 30th June, 1960.
Revd Alan Newman

BR Standard class '5' 4-6-0 No. 73068 fitted with speedometer, beside the water softener *c.*1963.
R.J. Cannon/Author's Collection

Ex-GWR 4-6-0 No. 6956 *Mottram Hall* in the ex-S&D shed on 28th August, 1965. It had arrived with a pigeon special.   *Revd Alan Newman*

'47') No. D1963 worked the 6.25 pm Bath to Avonmouth freight on one occasion, while latterly 'Westerns' and 'Hymeks' hauled some stopping trains. On 23rd February, 1966 a 'Warship' worked the 7.25 am to Temple Meads, normally a 'Hymek' turn.

Following closure to passenger traffic, freight trains were operated by engines of the 'Warship', 'Hymek', Brush and 'D95XX' classes based at Bristol Bath Road Depot.

Table One

LOADING OF PASSENGER AND FREIGHT ENGINES 1ST OCTOBER, 1945

Bath-Mangotsfield *Class of Engine*	1P	2P	3P	4P	5P	5X	2F	3F	4F	5F
Tons	170	230	280	310	355	405	255	310	340	390
Mangotsfield-Bath										
Tons	200	270	325	360	415	470	295	360	395	455

LOADING OF MINERAL TRAINS

Bath-Mangotsfield Class of engine	1	2	3	4	5	6	7	8
No. of wagons	28	34	40	48	53	58	64	70
Mangotsfield-Bath								
No. of wagons	30	36	43	52	57	63	69	76

Note: Maximum number of wagons authorised in either direction was 50.

Table Two

BATH (INCLUDING RADSTOCK) LOCOMOTIVE ALLOCATIONS

10th November, 1945 (22C)

Class '1P' 0-4-4T:	1324, 1334, 1348
Class '2P' 4-4-0:	497, 518, 696, 697, 700
Class '3P' 2-6-2T:	115, 181
Class '5P5F' 4-6-0:	4844, 5056, 5440
Sentinel 0-4-0T:	7191
Class '0F' 0-4-0ST:	11202
Class '3F' 0-6-0:	3734
Class '3F' 0-6-0T:	7275, 7316, 7465, 7496, 7542, 7557
Class '4F' 0-6-0:	3875, 4096, 4102, 4402, 4523, 4557, 4558, 4559, 4560, 4561
Class '7F' 2-8-0:	13800, 13801, 13802, 13803, 13804, 13805, 13806, 13807, 13808, 13809, 13810

Total: 43

'Western' class diesel-hydraulic No. D1039 *Western King* at the entrance to the coal yard sidings c.1967. *R.J. Cannon/Author's Collection*

Diesel-hydraulic 0-6-0 No. D9521 with a train at Midland Bridge Road yard, 1st April, 1966. *Revd Alan Newman*

1st November, 1954 (71G)
Class '2P' 4-4-0:   40568, 40569, 40601, 40696, 40697, 40698, 40700
Class '2MT' 2-6-2T: 41241, 41242, 41243
Class '5MT' 4-6-0:   44917, 45440, 73050, 73051, 73052
Sentinel 0-4-0T: 47190, 47191
Class '3F' 0-6-0T: 47275, 47316, 47465, 47496, 47542, 47557
Class '4F' 0-6-0:   44096, 44422, 44523, 44557, 44558, 44559, 44560, 44561
Class '7F' 2-8-0   53800, 53801, 53802, 53803, 53804, 53805, 53806, 53807, 53808
                        53809, 53810

Total: 42

May 1965 (82F)
Class '3MT' 2-6-2T: 82004, 82041
Class '5MT'4-6-0:   73001, 73051, 73054, 73068
Class '3F' 0-6-0T: 47276, 47506, 47544
Class '4F' 0-6-0   44558
Class '8F' 2-8-0   48309, 48444, 48525, 48660, 48737
Class '57XX' 0-6-0PT: 3681, 3758
Class '94XX' 0-6-0PT: 8436, 8486

Total: 19

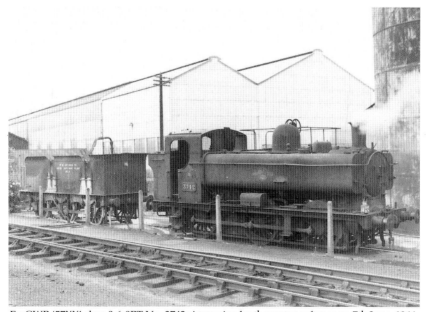

Ex-GWR '57XX' class 0-6-0PT No. 3742 simmering by the water softener on 7th June, 1964.
To the left is a sludge tender bearing the notice: 'To be returned to Water Softening Plant
Bath'.   *Author*

Bath motive power depot viewed from the top of the water softener, 1938.

Chapter Eight

Bath Motive Power Depot

West of the river bridge near Bath station was the stone-built MR shed opened in 1869. A 42 ft diameter turntable was provided and a timber-built coal stage. In preparation for the anticipated arrival of the S&D at Bath on 20th July, 1874, on 5th May the Midland had accepted the tender of Samuel Robertson of Bristol for building an independent two-road shed of timber. It had a height of 19 ft and measured 160 ft by 30 ft. A coal stage constructed of timber and brick was built immediately to the north (10 years later it was converted to a fitters' and blacksmith's shop). Traffic increased to such an extent that the shed was quite inadequate to handle the number of S&D locomotives, so Robertson was called in to add an almost identical engine shed to the south of the original S&D shed. As the Midland turntable had to be removed to make room for this extension, the opportunity was taken to replace it by a slightly larger one of 46 ft, this being used jointly by the MR and S&D. In 1883-4 the S&D shed frontage was equalised by the first shed being lengthened about 100 ft and the second by 56 ft. At the same time a new coaling stage was built adjacent to the southern approach road. This stage was rebuilt in 1954. Following the 1929 runaway caused by the crew being overcome by fumes in Combe Down tunnel (*see Chapter Eleven*), Welsh, rather than North Country coal was used at Bath, this giving out rather less fumes. Bedwas coal was particularly popular for its heating properties. (Further details of the S&D shed at Bath can be found in *Highbridge in its Heyday* by Colin G. Maggs, published by Oakwood Press.)

The fitting shop received electricity in 1909 to provide power for the dc motor which drove three lathes, two drillers, a shaper and grindstone through a system of overhead shafts and belts. In January 1934 a balancing table for weighing locomotives was installed.

In 1928 supervision of the former Midland depot was placed under the control of the S&D locomotive superintendent. The staff still used the old MR depot, but signed on and off at the S&D locomotive office. After 1st January, 1930 the MR running shed was reserved for engines under extended repairs. The S&D shed was set at a lower level than the MR line, which was on an embankment, and so was sometimes flooded, for example on 5th December, 1960. The steep gradient from the shed led to slipping, particularly if a dead engine was being hauled out. In 1948 the steam breakdown crane was the 15 ton type RS 1022 built in 1893.

The MR shed, a sub of Bristol and sharing the same Code 8, in 1930 became 8 (S&D); five years later it was recoded 22C; on 2nd February, 1948 when the Southern Region took over it became 71G and on 1st February, 1958 82F when ownership passed to the Western Region.

Although the first S&D 2-8-0s had been constructed in 1914, twenty years later it was still not possible to turn these engines at Bath. As the bridge replacement programme of the 1930s would allow longer engines to run over the line from Mangotsfield, a larger turntable was essential, so a 60 ft turntable was installed in February 1935 at a cost of about £3,375. When the turntable was out of operation,

Ex-MR shed with class '2P' 4-4-0 No. 505 (21A, Saltley) and 0-4-0ST No. 11202 in evidence *c.*1935.
Author's Collection

Bath ex-MR shed *c.*1964: 'Peak' class diesel-electric *left*; BR Standard class '3' 2-6-2T No. 82041; class '4F' 0-6-0 No. 44146 and an unidentified class '4F'.   *Dr T.R.N. Edwards*

Rear view of Bath MPD *c.*1966: ex-MR shed left, tank house and ex-S&D shed, right. The 'Boat Road' and quay for rail/water interchange is on the far bank. *C. Steane*

Rear view of ex-MR shed from the south-east in February 1967 following the lifting of track in the foreground which led to the passenger station. Notice the typical MR buffer stop - a corral of vertical sleepers bound with rail and filled with earth. *C. Steane*

Bath MPD on 28th March, 1959. The water softener, left with class '2P' 4-4-0s Nos. 40700 and 40569, ex-S&D shed *centre*; class '7F' 2-8-0 No. 53802 in front of the coal stage, *centre right* and part of the ex-MR shed on the far right.   *Author*

Two ex-SR engines at Bath: 'U' class 2-6-0 No. 31639 and an air-smoothed Pacific.
Gordon Dando Collection

Above: A class '7F' 2-8-0 on the new Cowans, Sheldon & Co. 60 ft diameter turntable, February 1935.

Bath Evening Chronicle

Right: Warning notice by the Bath turntable. *W.F. Grainger*

Below: Ex-S&DJR class '4F' 0-6-0 No. 44558 and BR Standard class '9' 2-10-0 No. 92214 at Bath on 7th June, 1964. The crew are winding the turntable around by hand. *Author*

NOTICE TO ENGINEMAN WHEN TURNING 2-10-0 ENGINES ON THIS TABLE GREAT CARE MUST BE TAKEN TO SEE THEY DO NOT FOUL WAGONS ON THE COAL ROAD

Class '4F' 0-6-0 No. 44523 *left* and class '7F' 2-8-0 No. 13805 pictured on 15th August, 1949. The
overhead gantry is for ash disposal.   *Author*

The ex-S&D shed flooded by water rising through a drain on 5th December, 1960. Only ash
wagons occupy the shed.   *John Stamp*

locomotives were turned on the triangle at Mangotsfield, up to eight being sent together. All the engines behind the first were 'dead' but had to be manned by a rider. On a cold day he placed a shovel of fire on the baffle plate to keep himself warm. Mangotsfield triangle was also used for turning the 7.05 pm Bristol to Newcastle mail vans as the pick-up apparatus was only on one side.

In the 1930s the points to turn an engine on to the Ash Road (officially No. 1, though never called this) by the coaling stage had to be held over - they would not remain set by themselves. To do this the operator had to lean towards the engine as it crossed the points. This was a highly dangerous thing to have to do and later a different pattern lever was installed. A gantry spanned the four shed roads for the removal of ash and smoke box char to the Ash Road. Although the gantry remained, the lift was not operational latterly, perhaps due to the dusty environment having a detrimental effect on its mechanism.

The first job on Monday morning for the relief men was to remove the wagon from the Ash Road to the Boat Road, drop pit men having filled the wagon over the weekend. Beside No. 2 Road was a booster pump for washing out boilers. This road was also used for filling the fuel tanks of oil burning locomotives from ordinary rail tankers held at the rear of the coal road, the large oil tank near the water softener never being used. No. 6 Road (though not referred to as this) ran to the fitting shop; the water softening plant was between Roads 8 and 9, a red brick building storing the soda used for water softening. Sludge from the softener was pumped into an old tender and taken by the 11.29 pm freight to Westerleigh, the loose-coupled vehicle being marshalled next to the brake van, it was then sent on to Coalville, Leicestershire, by slow freight. There were two such wagons, one always standing on No. 9 road, while the other was being emptied. The sludge pit, a 12 ft cube, had its contents discharged to the vehicle by dint of a cleaner turning a handle. The shed water supply was from a tank supplied by gravity from a spring in the S&D's Devonshire Tunnel, 4 and 6 inch pipes conveying the water to a tank at the locomotive shed. Additionally a well was sunk near the Boat Shed from which a two-throw ram pump transferred water into a 30,000 gallon tank.

The enginemen's mess room was situated outside the S&D shed at the rear of No. 3 Road - a very unsafe position for if an engine had come through the blocks, men would have been killed or injured. The cabin was out of bounds for the cleaners, so Mrs Steiner, who kept the cabin spruce, boiled eggs for them, after pencilling on their initials so their owners could claim them.

Ex-GWR 4-6-0 No. 7813 *Freshford Manor* at Bath on 13th May, 1961. It had arrived with a pigeon special. Class '4F' 0-6-0 No. 44139 (16A, Nottingham) is on the left. No. 44213 (21A, Saltley) is by the ex-MR shed.   *Revd Alan Newman*

Class '2P' 4-4-0 No. 509 (21A, Saltley) at Bath shed *c.*1936.   *Author's Collection*

Class '3F' 0-6-0T No. 47623 *c.*1963 with its front buffers removed and replaced by a snow plough.
Dr Christopher Kent

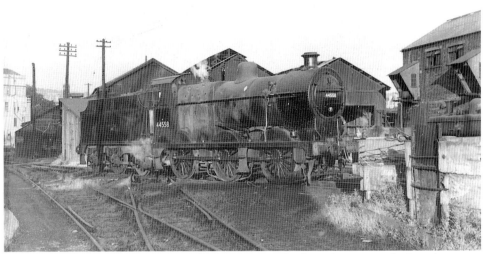

Ex-S&D class '4F' 0-6-0 No. 44558 on the Boat Road *c*.1960. The coal stage is on the far right.
Dr T.R.N. Edwards

Bath MPD on 6th March, 1966: ex-GWR 0-6-0PTs sandwich class '2' 2-6-2T No. 41206 *centre left*, two class '2' 2-6-2Ts and a class '3F' 0-6-0T. *C. Steane*

BR Standard class '9' 2-10-0 No. 92214 (82F, Bath) having its ashes raked out *c*.1960. To the right
is the coal stage and a pannier tank used for shunting duties.   *Dr T.R.N. Edwards*

BR Standard class '5' 4-6-0 No. 73082 *Camelot* (70A, Nine Elms) and class '7F' 2-8-0 No. 53807
(82F, Bath) on 27th March, 1964. the latter engine has 'Bath's Best' chalked on the smokebox
hinge.   *Revd Alan Newman*

Chapter Nine

Passenger Timetables and Push-Pull Working

Local Trains

The first passenger timetable for the service which began on 4th August, 1869 showed nine trains each way daily and four on Sundays, most taking 40 minutes from Bath to Bristol Temple Meads, but one each way covering the distance in half an hour, only stopping at Weston. This compared with the contemporary GWR times of 17 minutes (express) and 30 minutes (stopping). The MR mileage was 15 and that of the GWR 11½. MR fares were the same as those on the GWR, but the latter ran fewer third class trains. Competition certainly made itself felt, for a few days after the opening of the Midland branch to Bath, fares on GWR expresses Bath to Bristol were reduced to the ordinary rate. The GWR ran a service of 19 down and 20 up trains. In September 1869 the MR service increased to 13 each way, two running non-stop except for a call at Weston.

May 1870 saw the opening of St Philip's station at Bristol - the MR's own terminus - after which two extra trains were run, others accelerated and third class passenger accommodation provided on every train instead of only in about half of them. In June 1870 there were 10 stopping trains each way Bath to Bristol, most taking 35-40 minutes. One, only stopping at Weston, Bitton and Warmley, reached Temple Meads in 30 minutes; two short workings were run between Bath and Mangotsfield and three in the opposite direction. The Sunday service comprised four trains each way between Bath and St Philip's and one short working Bath to Mangotsfield and return. By August 1887 the service had increased to 15 each way daily, all running to St Philip's except the 11.10 pm which used Temple Meads. Only three trains ran each way on Sundays.

In April 1910, 18 trains ran from Bath to Bristol and 16 in the reverse direction, most using St Philip's, but some ran to Temple Meads including one travelling non-stop in 23 minutes and therefore averaging 39 mph. It connected with an express to York which did not pick up at Mangotsfield. There were two trains each way on Sundays which used Temple Meads and stopped at all stations except Kelston.

Bath station was busy around midday - the July 1914 timetable showed departures at 11.57 am to Birmingham; 12.05 pm express to Mangotsfield; 12.15 stopping passenger to Mangotsfield and 12.55 stopping passenger to Mangotsfield. Additionally trains ran into Bath from the S&D. This timetable showed one through train to Clifton Down. In July 1922 the local service comprised 15 trains from Bristol to Bath plus one from Clifton Down to Bitton and two from St Philip's to Bitton. Thirteen trains ran from Bath to Bristol plus one between Bitton and Mangotsfield only. One train ran between Bath and Temple Meads and vice versa only stopping at Fishponds and taking 32 minutes. The Sunday service consisted of two trains each way between Bath and Bristol.

By July 1938 an interesting service had developed. On weekdays there were 12 trains from St Philip's to Bath; four from Temple Meads including one through

BATH AND MANGOTSFIELD BRANCH.

BATH TO BRISTOL.

Mls. from Bath	STATIONS.	WEEK-DAYS.														
		1	2	3	4	5	6	7	8	9	11	12	12½	13	14	15
		Pass.	Pass.	Goods	Pass.	Pass.	Pass.	Light Engine	Pass.	Pass.	Pass.	Pass.	Light Engine	Goods &c.	Pass.	Pass.
		a.m.	a.m.	a. m.	a.m.	a.m.	a.m.	a. m.	a. m.	p. m.	p.m	p.m	p.m	p. m.	p.m.	p.m.
	BATH ....dep.	7 40	8 25	8 40	9 20	9 40	10 45	11 0	11 35	12 45	3 55	4 15	5 5	5 35	6 30	7 10
¾	Weston	7 43	8 28	8 50	9 23	9 43	10 48	..	11 38	12 48	3 58	4 18	..	6 35	6 33	7 13
4	Keiston	..	8 35	..	..	..	..	..	12 55	..	..	..	..	6 40	..	
6¼	Bitton	7 53	8 41	9 15	9 33	9 52	10 53	..	11 43	1 3	3 4	4 23	..	6 50	6 46	7 23
8¼	Warmley	7 58	8 46	9 25	9 38	9 58	11 3	..	11 53	1 6	3 13	4 33	..	6 0	6 51	7 26
10¼	MANGOTSFIELD { arr. dep.	8 1	8 5	..	..	10 4	11 9	6 11	11 57	1 10	3 16	4 36	5 20	6 6	6 55	7 32
12½	Fish Ponds............	8 8	8 53	..	..	10 4	11 9	..	..	1 13	1 14	4 39	..	..	6 58	
15½	BRISTOL, Temple Mid. arr	8	8 5	..	..	10 20	..	..	..	1 18	2 14	4 41	..	7 3		
	Ditto. St. Philip's ..	8	8 59	..	..	9 50	..	11 20	..	..	1 25	3 0	4 40	..	7 10	

Mls. from Bath	STATIONS.	WEEK-DAYS.									SUNDAYS				
		16	17	18	19	20	21	22	23	24	25	26	27	28	29	30
		Goods	Pass.								Pass.	Pass.	Pass.	Pass.	Pass.
		p. m.	p.m.								a.m.	p. m.	p.m.	p.m.	p.m
	BATH ....dep.	7 25	8 15	..	..	..	..	..	..	..	9 15	1 45	4 25	6 30	8 30
¾	Weston	7 17	8 18	..	..	..	..	..	..	..	9 18	1 48	4 28	6 33	8 33
4	Keiston	..	..	..	..	..	..	..	..	..	9 25	1 55	4 35	6 40	8 40
6¼	Bitton	7 48	8 25	..	..	..	..	..	..	..	9 31	2 1	4 41	6 46	8 46
8¼	Warmley	7 53	8 33	..	..	..	..	..	..	..	9 37	2 7	4 46	6 51	8 42
10¼	MANGOTSFIELD { arr. dep.	8	8 37 / 8 38	..	..	..	..	..	..	..	9 41 / 9 42	2 11 / 2 12	4 50	6 55 / 6 58	8 54 / 8 57
12½	Fish Ponds............	..	8 43	..	..	..	..	..	..	..	9 43	2 13	..	7 3	9 3
15½	BRISTOL, Temple Md. arr	..	..	..	..	..	..	..	..	..	..	..	..		
	Ditto. St. Philip's ..	8 20	8 50	..	..	..	..	..	..	..	9 55	2 25	..	7 10	9 10

6 Train stops at Keiston on Thursdays.

BRISTOL TO BATH.

Miles from Bristol	STATIONS.	WEEK-DAYS.														
		31	32	33	34	35	36	37	38	39	40	41	42	43	44	45
		Goods	Pass.	Pass.	Pass.	Goods	Pass.	Goods	Pass.	Pass.	Pass.	Pass.	Pass.	Pass.	Pass.	Goods
		a. m.	a.m.	a. m.	a.m.	a.m.	a.m.	a. m.	a. m.	p.m.	p.m	p.m	p.m	p.m.	p.m.	p. m.
	BRISTOL, St. Philip's dep	6 10	7 10	8 25	9 20	..	..	10 45	..	11 50	..	2 0	4 15	5 10	..	6 10
	Ditto. Temple Md. ,,	..	..	..	..	..	10 45	..	11 57	..	2 7	4 22	5 17	..	6 17	
3	Fish Ponds	6 18	7 17	8 42	..	..	10 52	..	12 ..	..	2 12	4 27	5 21	..	6 22	
5	MANGOTSFIELD { arr. dep.	6 25 / 6 30	7 21 / 7 22	8 46 / 8 47	9 29 / 9 30	9 45	10 57	11 15	12 2 / 12 12	12 7	2 14	4 30	5 22	5 27	6 28	6 50
7	Warmley	6 41	7 26	8 51	9 34	10 0	11 1	..	..	12 16	5 26	5 31	5 36	6 27		
9¼	Bitton	6 46	7 31	8 56	9 39	10 10	11 6	..	12 10	12 16	2 23	4 40	5 31	5 36	6 32	
11¼	Keiston	..	..	9 41	..	10 17	..	12 20	12 25	2 37	5 15	5 41	5 46			
14¼	Weston	7 41	9 6	9 51	10 30	11 17	..	12 25	12 30	4 40	5 55	5 50	6 50	7 6		
15½	BATH .... arr.	7 5	7 45	9 10	9 55	10 35	11 20	12 10	12 25	12 30	4 40	5 55	5 50	6 50	7 5	

Miles from Bristol	STATIONS.	WEEK-DAYS									SUNDAYS				
		46	47	48	49	50	51	52	53	54	55	56	57	58	59	60
		Pass.	Pass.								Pass.	Pass.	Pass.	Pass.	Pass.
		p. m.	p. m.								a.m.	a.m.	p.m.	p.m.	p. m.
	BRISTOL, St. Philip's dep	..	8 0	..	..	..	..	..	..	..	8 15	11 15	2 45	..	7 30
	Ditto. Temple Md. ,,	..	..	..	..	..	..	..	..	..	..	..	..	..	
3	Fish Ponds	..	8 7	..	..	..	..	..	..	..	8 22	11 22	2 52	..	7 37
5	MANGOTSFIELD { arr. dep.	7 41	8 11 / 8 12	..	..	..	..	..	..	..	8 27 / 8 28	11 37 / 11 37	2 57 / 2 58	5 5	7 42 / 7 43
7	Warmley	7 45	8 16	..	..	..	..	..	..	..	8 33	11 32	3 3	5 7	7 47
9¼	Bitton	7 56	8 21	..	..	..	..	..	..	..	8 37	11 37	3 7	5 14	7 52
11¼	Keiston	..	..	..	..	..	..	..	..	..	8 43	11 43	3 13	5 20	7 58
14¼	Weston	8 0	8 31	..	..	..	..	..	..	..	8 51	11 51	3 21	5 27	8 6
15½	BATH .... arr.	8 5	8 35	..	..	..	..	..	..	..	8 55	11 55	3 25	5 30	8 10

42 Train stops at Keiston on Thursdays.

Working Timetable for the line, June 1870.

MANGOTSFIELD AND BATH.

WEEKDAYS.

Distance from Mangotsfield Sta.	STATIONS.	1	1a	2	3	4	5	6	7	8	9	10	11	12	13	14
		S. & D. Goole.		S. & D. Goole.	11.56 a.m. Mineral from Bristol.	S. & D. Goole.	S. & D. Goole.	2.0 a.m. Mineral from Westerleigh.	1.30 a.m. Mineral Tuesdays excepted.	S. & D. Goole.			3.30 a.m. Stop Freight from Bristol.	3.34 a.m. Stops if Freight from Bristol.	S. & D. Goole.
		a.m.		a.m.	a.m.	a.m.	a.m.	a.m.	a.m.	a.m.			a.m.	a.m.	a.m.
..	MANGOTSF'LD STATION dep.	Q		Q	M	M	Q	Sop. 384.	M				M	MO	M
..	M'ngtsfld N.Jn.							57					4 25	4 25	
1¾	Warmley						Tudys only.						4 40	4 40	
3¾	Bitton								Stops at Warmley Mornings.				4 40	4 40	
6¾	Kelston														
9	Weston.... arr. / dep.												4 55 / 5 10		
9½	Bath Junct { arr. / dep.			1 12			2 32		3 22				5 12 / 5 40	4 55	
10	BATH arr.	1 0		1 28	1 40	1 43	2 31	3 0	3 18	3 55	4 17		5 42		5 55

	STATIONS	15	16	17	18	19	20	21	22	22a	23	24	25	26	27	28	30
		Light Engine from Westerleigh	Fish.	S. & D. Goole.	Passenger ex Bristol.	10.35 p.m. Mineral from Birmingham.	S. & D. Passenger	Passenger 7.10 a.m. ex Bristol.	Engine Brake.		S. & D. Goole.	S. & D. Passenger	8.20 a.m. Mineral ex Bristol (St. P.)	Express Gloucester.	Passenger 8.54 a.m. from Clifton Down.	S. & D. Passenger	S. & D. Passenger
		a.m.	a.m.	a.m.	a.m.	a.m.	a.m.	a.m.	a.m.	a.m.	a.m.	a.m.	a.m.	a.m.	a.m.	a.m.	a.m.
	MANGOTSFIELD STATION..dep.	M	M	M	6 19	M	7 59	8†40			9 16			10 5			
	Mangotsfield N. Jn.	EW17		5 55			7 37						9 45				
	Warmley				6 23	P	8 3				9 20				10012		
	Bitton	5 25			6A29		8 8	8 47			9 25				10012		
	Kelston						8 13				9 30						
	Weston arr. / dep.						8 18 / 8 20		Mangotsfield South.		9 35 / 9 38						
	Bath Junction.. arr. / dep.				8 13												
	BATH arr.	6 10	6 30	6 30	8 16	8 17	8 23			9 10	9 27	9 41	10 1	10 5	10 21	10 27	11 32

	STATIONS.	31	32	33	34	35 – 36	37	38	39	40	41	42	45	46	47	48
		S. & D. Passenger.	Passenger ex Bristol.	S. & D. Passenger	8.45 a.m. Mineral from Gloucester.	S. & D. Passenger	8. & D. Goole.	Passenger ex Bristol.	Express.	S. & D. Goole.	1.35 p.m. Stops Freight Westerleigh.	S. & D. Passenger	Passenger ex Bristol.	Express 2.12 p.m. (from Derby) Bristol (T.M.)	Express 12.50 p.m. from Derby.	S. & D. Passenger.
		a.m.	a.m.	p.m.	a.m.	p.m.	p.m.	p.m.	p.m.	p.m.	p.m.	p.m.	p.m.	p.m.	p.m.	p.m.
	MANGOTSFIELD STATION..dep.		11 45	Y	11 55		1 32		S			2 58	3 33		3 45		
	Mangotsfield N. Jn.							55				3 2					
	Warmley		11 49		12 10		1 36				2 18	3 2	7	3B40			
	Bitton		11 54				1 41					3 12					
	Kelston		12E 0				1 46					3 17					
	Weston arr. / dep.						1 51 / 1 53					3 19					
	Bath Junction.. arr. / dep.				12 30 / 12 52		1 56					3 2	3 23		4 0		
	BATH arr.	11 50	12 7	12 34	12 53	1 30	1 56	2 2	2 42	47		3 2	3 23	3 49	4 0	4 20	

	STATIONS.	49	50	51	52	54	55	56	59	60	61	62	63	64	65	66
		S. & D. Goole.	4.0 p.m. Mineral from Bristol.	Passenger ex Bristol.	3.54 a.m. Thro. Wathrwell'th	Express 3.24 (to Bath) (T.M.)	S. & D. Passenger	Express Gloucester to N. Jct.	Passenger 4.22 p.m. ex Bristol.	S. & D. Goole.	5.35 p.m. Mineral from Westerleigh	Passenger ex Bristol.	S. & D. Passenger	6.33 p.m. Mineral ex Bristol.	S. & D. Coal from Radstock.	5.30 p.m. Mineral from Gloucester.
		p.m.	p.m.	p.m.	p.m.	p.m.	p.m.	p.m.	p.m.	p.m.	p.m.	p.m.	p.m.	p.m.	p.m.	p.m.
	MANGOTSFIELD STATION..dep.	MO Q	4 16	4 57	MS	5 36		5 42	6 7	Y	6 46		6 50		X	MO V
	Mangotsfield N. Jun.				5						6 11					6 50
	Warmley		5 1						6 11		6 50		6 55			7 25
	Bitton		5 6						6 16		6 55		7 0			
	Kelston		5 11						6 21		7 0		7 5			
	Weston arr. / dep.		5 17 / 5 19						6 27 / 6 29		7 5		7 8			
	Bath Junction arr. / dep.		4 42 / 5 23	5 30		5 50		5 58	6 326		6 35		7 15			7 45 / 8 2
	BATH arr.	6 15	5 25	6 22		5 50	6 58	6 1	6 326 65		7 12		7 20		7 44	8 10

A—Arrives Bitton at 8.17 a.m.   B—Arrive Bitton at 3.25 p.m.   D—Arrives Bitton at 10.16.
E—Arrives at Kelston at 11.56 a.m.   F—Commences running July.10th.
V—Detaches cattle where required.   X—Attaches traffic for Southampton at Warmley, when required.
Y—Detaches cattle where required.

Working Timetable for the line, July 1914.

BATH AND MANGOTSFIELD.

WEEKDAYS.

Distance	STATIONS.	39 Passenger	40 S. & D. Passenger	41 Express to Gloucester	42 S. & D. Goods	43 Express to Bristol (M.J.)	44 S. & D. Goods	46 Express to Birmingham	47 Express (Saturdays only).	48 Express to Flutheld	49 Express	51 Passenger	53 S. & D. Passenger	53 Express	54 S. & D. Goods.
Miles		a. m.	a.m.	a.m.	a.m.	a.m.	a.m.	a.m.	a.m.	a.m.	p.m.	p.m.	p.m.	p.m.	p.m.
..	BATH ....dep.	9 50	10 28	10 32	10 50	10 40	11 50	11 57	11 57	12 5	12 15	12 14	12 40	12 40
1	Weston	9 53									12 18			
..	Shaw & Co.'s Siding..													
4¼	Kelston	9 59									12 25			
6¼	Bitton	10 4			10 50						12 30			
8¼	Warmley	(10 10)									12 35			
10¼	Mangotsfield Jun.			10 45										
10	MANGOTSFIELD STATION arr.	10 13			10 55					12 22	12 39		12 54	

STATIONS.	58 Passenger	59 S. & D. Passenger	60 S. & D. Goods	61 Passenger	62 Through Freight to Gloucester	63 S. & D. Passenger	64 S. & D. Passenger	65 S. & D. & oods.	66 Sleeping Freight to Westerleigh	68	69 Express to Sheaail.	71 S. & D. Goods.	72 Passenger	73 S. & D. Passenger	77 Passenger.	78
	p.m.	p.m.	p.m.	p.m.	p.m.	p.m.	p.m.	p.m.	p.m.	p.m.	p.m.	p.m.	p.m.	p.m.	p.m.	p.m.
BATH ....dep.	12 55	1 27	1 40	1 45	2 0	2 13	2 23	2 55	S	3 15	3 15	3 40	4 0	4 5	4 35	4 40
Weston	12 59			1 48									4 3			4 50
Shaw & Co.'s Siding..																
Kelston				1 54									4 9			
Bitton	1 8			1 59			3 5						4 16			
Warmley	1 13			2 5			4 10						4 22			5 27
Mangotsfield N. Jun.				2 38				4 15			3 A 5					
MANGOTSFIELD STATION arr.	1 17			2 8					3 31				4 25		4 43	

STATIONS.	80 S. & D. Passenger	81 S. & D. Goods.	84 Passenger	85 Through Freight to Westerleigh	88 S. & D. Passenger	89 Passenger to Bristol	90 S. & D. Goods.	91 Through Freight to Westerleigh	92 Through Freight to Westerleigh	93 Through Freight to Sharpness.	93A S. & D. Goods.	94 Passenger	95 Through Freight to Water Orton.	96 S. & D. Passenger	97 S. & D. Goods.
	p.m.	p.m.	p.m.	p.m.	p.m.	p.m.	p.m.	p.m.	S	SO	p.m.	p.m.	p.m.	p.m.	p.m.
BATH .... dep.	4 55	5 20	5	5 45	6	6 30	6 35	6 45	7 0	7 15	7 20	7 40	7 55	8 0	8 5
Weston			5 33	SO	6 33								SO		Q
Shaw & Co.'s Siding..															
Kelston			5 39		6 39										
Bitton			5 44	6 15	6 44			7 28				7 51			
Warmley			5 50	6 35	6 50			8 10							
Mangotsfield N. Jn.								7 5		7 40					
MANGOTSFIELD STATION arr.			5 53		6 53							7 58			

STATIONS.	99 S. & D. Goods.	100 Through Freight to Birmingham (To Saturdays).	103 S. & D. Goods.	104 Passenger	105	106 Through Freight to Westerleigh (To Saturdays Mondays)	107 S. & D. Goods.	108 S. & D. Passenger	110 Mineral to Buttswood.	113 Passenger to Bristol (Temple Mead)	114 Mineral to Bristol.	116 Empty Carriages.	117 S. & D. Goods.	119 Mineral to Birmingham.
	p.m.	p.m.	p.m.	p.m.		p.m.	p.m.	p.m.	SO	p.m.	p.m.	p.m.	p.m.	p.m.
BATH .... dep.	8 40	8 50	9 34	9 40		9 45	10 5	10 30	10 55	11 0	11 15	SO	11 25	11 45
Weston		Z				S	Q							MO
Shaw & Co.'s Siding..														
Kelston	Q			9 51						B	S	11 55		
Bitton				9 57										
Warmley									11 0					
Mangotsfield N. Jn.										11 15	11 42	12 5		
MANGOTSFIELD STATION arr.			10 0											

A—Passes Mangotsfield South Junction at 3.29 p.m.
B—Stops at Bitton and Warmley on Saturdays, and arrives Mangotsfield at 11.18.
D—Runs 5 mins. later on Mondays and Saturdays.
E—Stops at Kelston on Saturdays.
U—Attaches through Manchester wagons or Manchester tariff at Warmley, when required.
Z—Conveys mail bags Bath to Westerleigh. On Saturdays attaches through Manchester wagons or Manchester tariff at Warmley.

Working Timetable for the line, July 1914.

WEEKDAYS.

	STATIONS.	67	68	69	70	71	72	75	76	77	78	79	80	81	82
		p.m	p.m	p.m	p.m	p.m	p.m.	p.m.	p.m.	p.m.		p.m.	p.m.	p.m.	p.m.
..	MANGOTSFIELD STATION..dep.	7 58		SO		S	0 15	9 43		..		..	11 37	SO	..
1¼	Mangotsfield N. Jur.														
1¼	Warmley	8 2		8 5			9A20	9 47					11 41		..
3½	Bitton	8 7					9A27	9053					11 45		..
6½	Kelston	8 12													..
9	Weston arr.	8 17						..							
	Weston dep.	8 19						..							
9½	Bath Junction arr.			8 25		9 2			10 27		10 33				
	Bath Junction dep.			8 65		9 43				11 3					
10	BATH arr.	8 22	8 60	9 0	9 30	9 45	9 38	10 3	10 11		11 6			11 17	11 56

SUNDAYS.

STATIONS.	1	2	3	4	5	6	7	8	9	10	11	12	13	14	16	18	19	20
	a.m	a.m.	a.m.	a.m.	a.m.	a.m.	a.m.	a.m.	a.m.	a.m.	a.m.	a.m.	a.m.	a.m.	a.m.	a.m.	p.m.	p.m.
MANGOTSFIELD STATION..dep.											9 17	6 30	10 17			9 4		10 20
Mangotsfield N. Jun.								3 0	5 3				10 21		9 8			
Warmley													10 26		9 13			
Bitton																		
Kelston																		
Weston arr.								5 23	5 50				10 37		9 24			
Weston dep.								5 33	6 0				10 39		9 26			
Bath Junction arr.				1 10				3 20		5 35	6 3			12 3			10 45
Bath Junction dep.				1 43				3 45		6 3	6 33			12 29			10 57
BATH arr.	12 22	0 1	28	43	45 2	7 2	3 13	3 43	50	4 66	5 35	6 45	10 42	12 30	0 29	10 30	11 0

A—Arrives Warmley at 9.10 and Bitton at 9.24 p.m.   D—Arrives at Bitton at 9.31.

BATH AND MANGOTSFIELD.

WEEKDAYS.

	STATIONS.	1	3	6	9	11	12	13	14	15	16	17	19
Miles		a.m.	a.m.	a.m.	a.m.	a.m.	a.m.		a.m.	a.m.	a.m.		a.m.
..	BATH dep.	12 30	12 40	1 20	2 50	3 30	3 35	..	4 40	6 30	M	2 10	5 50
1	Weston	M			..		M	..	M				
..	Shaw & Co.'s Siding												
4½	Kelston												
6½	Bitton										8 30	8 30	
8½	Warmley												
10½	Mangotsfield N. Jun.												
10	MANGOTSFIELD STATION... arr.												

STATIONS.	19	23	24	25	26	27	28	31	32	34	37	38
	a.m.	a.m.	a.m.	a.m.	a.m.	a.m.	a.m.	a.m.	a.m.		a.m.	a.m.
BATH dep.	6 45	6 50	6 55	7 30	7 35	7 48	8 30	8 37	8 46	..	9 35	
Weston	M	7 0			7 36		Q	8 40				
Shaw & Co.'s Siding		7 10										
Kelston								8 46				
Bitton		7 30			7 43			8 51				9 30
Warmley		6 16			7 55	8 1		6 57			10 0	10 15
Mangotsfield N. Jun.											10 0	10 25
MANGOTSFIELD STATION arr.	7 10	7 40			7 59	8 4		9 0				

Working Timetable for the line, July 1914.

Class '1P' 0-4-4T No. 1328 at Mangotsfield on a train to Bath *c*.1925. This engine has only two coal rails to its bunker.   *S. Miles Davey*

Class '1P' 0-4-4T No. 1334 accelerates from Kelston station with an up stopping train in the 1930s.   *S. Miles Davey*

stopping train to Bournemouth West and one through express to Bournemouth West. Three trains started from Clifton Down, two of which ran through to Bournemouth West and there were two short workings - one from Temple Meads to Bitton and one from Mangotsfield to Bath. In the reverse direction there were 15 trains from Bath to St Philip's including one with through coaches from Bournemouth West; three to Temple Meads including one express with through coaches from Bournemouth West; one to Clifton Down and one from Bitton to Clifton Down. The Sunday service consisted of four trains from Temple Meads to Bath, one of which was a through express to Bournemouth West; and five from Bath to Temple Meads including two expresses from Bournemouth West.

An interesting innovation in World War II was motor trains, crews being sent to the Stroud and Nailsworth branch to learn push-pull working. On weekdays a set left Bath at 6.55 am for Bristol, St Philip's; then formed a workmen's service to Yate and Wickwar, returning as empty coaching stock to Lawrence Hill, Bristol. At 4.20 pm it left as empty coaching stock for Wickwar, collected workers from Yate and stations *en route* to St Philip's, finally leaving at 8.15 pm for Bath.

The Sunday service left Bath at 7.25 am using Temple Meads as St Philip's was closed that day. Morning and afternoon trips were made to Bath before returning to Wickwar and Yate. It returned from Temple Meads to Bath and made a return evening trip to Mangotsfield.

In November 1944 the weekday service consisted of 10 trains each way from Bristol to Bath and on Sundays two from Bristol to Bath plus one from Mangotsfield to Bath; in the opposite direction one ran from Bath to Bristol and two from Bath to Mangotsfield. By January 1947 the service had improved to 14 each way from Bristol to Bath plus one Bristol to Bitton and back; two each way on Sundays and one from Mangotsfield to Bath and two Bath to Mangotsfield. In the summer timetable of 1954 the fastest train Temple Meads to Green Park was the 9.30 am through to Bournemouth West. Stopping only at Fishponds, Staple Hill and Mangotsfield, it covered the 15 miles in 32 minutes. Sometimes on summer Saturdays this train was piloted in order to get an engine to Bath to head an express.

The summer timetable for 1959 showed 11 stopping trains from Bristol to Bath and two each way on Sundays, that is, two less than the previous year. Ten trains ran from Bath to Bristol, four of these departing between 6.20-8.11 am, but none leaving on weekdays after 7.03 pm and this latter running non-stop to Mangotsfield, the last stopping train departing at 6.18 pm, later passengers having to use a bus. This 7.03 pm, which was a through train from Bournemouth West, had a van behind the engine. At Mangotsfield the locomotive uncoupled, drew forward, the banker from Bristol taking the van and waiting with it in Tar Pot Siding (on the up side west of the station), later attaching it to the 7.20 pm Bristol to Newcastle mail. Meanwhile the engine from Bath had backed on to the coaches and proceeded to Bristol.

From 5th March, 1962 all services in the Bristol area were reduced as it was found that trains were running with many empty seats. The Bristol to Bath service was curtailed to seven each way and the Sunday service withdrawn. Until this date, a notice outside Green Park station read: 'This station is open on Sundays from 7.30 am to 11.30 am and 6.30 pm to 7.30 pm. When closed, enquiries can be made at Bath Spa station'.

Class '3P' 2-6-2T No. 180 at Bath in June 1941 with a train for Bristol St Philip's.
Colin Roberts Collection

The last train to Bristol, St Philip's which called at Weston station leaves behind class '2' 2-6-2T No. 41241 on 19th September, 1953. *Author*

Ex-GWR twin diesel railcars Nos. W35 and W36 with an intermediate trailer passing Bath Junction *c*.1954, working the 6.18 pm Green Park to Temple Meads. *F. Basil Robbins*

Ex-GWR diesel railcar No. 24W passing Newton Meadows with the 7.45 am Temple Meads to Green Park on a misty 27th March, 1954. *Author*

Class '2' 2-6-0 No. 46494 at Newton Meadows, passing mile post 132½ and a cattle creep with the 7.45 am Temple Meads to Green Park, 22nd August, 1955. This class of locomotive was unusual on a local passenger train. *Author*

Ex-GWR '45XX' class 2-6-2T No. 4572 at Newbridge, Bath, with the 6.18 pm Green Park to Temple Meads on 28th May, 1957. This train was normally worked by an ex-GWR engine or diesel railcar. *Author*

Ex-GWR '94XX' class 0-6-0PT No. 9481 west of Bath with the 6.18 pm Green Park to Temple Meads service on 3rd June, 1957.   *Author*

An ex-GWR '57XX' class 0-6-0PT No. 9795, also seen west of Bath with the 6.18 pm Green Park to Temple Meads service on 10th June, 1957.   *Author*

A Green Park to Temple Meads train hauled by a BR Standard class '3' 2-6-2T approaching Mangotsfield.   *D. Payne*

BR Standard class '3' 2-6-2T No. 82033 passes Bath Junction with the 6.18 pm Green Park to Temple Meads on 14th August, 1959. Ex-S&D class '4F' 0-6-0 No. 44559 can be seen left.   *Author*

Class '2' 2-6-2T No. 41248, formerly shedded at Kentish Town, with a Temple Meads to Green Park stopping train, enters Bitton on 28th April, 1962.   *R.E. Toop*

BR Standard class '3' 2-6-2T No. 82004 approaches Mangotsfield with a Bristol Temple Meads to Bath Green Park stopping train, 28th April, 1962.   *R.E. Toop*

'Hymek' diesel-hydraulic No. D7025 on the centre road. A locking bar to prevent the points being moved under a train may be seen towards the lower left-hand corner.

Author's Collection

Diesel-hydraulic 'Hymek' No. D7000 with the 13.00 Saturdays-only Green Park to Temple Meads on the last day of passenger service 5th March, 1966, seen here just west of Bath.

Author

Express Trains

From the opening of the S&D's Bath extension on 20th July, 1874, two trains carried through coaches to and from Birmingham. In 1876 through coaches to Bournemouth West were introduced from Bradford, Leeds and Sheffield as well as York and Newcastle. Other interesting trains were a Bradford to Plymouth train via Templecombe which ran between 1889-91; a service from Bournemouth West to Harrogate, 1904; and another from Bournemouth West to Worcester, 1907. From 1st July, 1909 a new corridor express ran through from Bath to Bradford Exchange via the MR and Lancashire & Yorkshire Railway (LYR). On 1st October, 1910 the precursor of the 'Pines Express' was introduced to run via the LNWR between Manchester and Birmingham, over the Midland to Bath and onwards via the S&D to Bournemouth. Suspended during World War I, the Leeds and Bradford through coaches were continued after the war.

The July 1922 timetable showed three expresses each way between Birmingham and Bournemouth West; one started from Liverpool Lime Street and Manchester London Road to Bournemouth West, also conveying coaches Manchester to Swanage and a restaurant car Birmingham to Bath. This train was closely followed by one from Bradford, Leeds, Lincoln and Nottingham to Bournemouth West, with a restaurant car facility between Sheffield and Bournemouth. These trains also ran in the reverse direction, the Birmingham to Bournemouth train returning to Bradford, S&D stock working this and getting quite far from home territory. In 1927 the Manchester to Bournemouth train was named the 'Pines Express'. Two years later a train was introduced from Nottingham to Sidmouth, Budleigh Salterton and Exmouth.

The title of the 'Pines Express' was suspended during World War II but restored in 1949, it conveying a Sheffield portion which ran as a separate train at summer weekends. The engine of the 12.40 am parcels from Leicester to Bath normally worked back to Gloucester with the up 'Pines', returned to Bath with the down 'Pines' and finished its day with the 8.25 pm perishables from Templecombe to Derby. In September 1953 four through trains ran from Bristol to Bournemouth and two in the reverse direction. In the summer of 1958, 12 extra Friday night/Saturday trains ran each way between the Midlands and Bournemouth. The Friday night down trains had the double advantage of giving passengers virtually an extra day at the seaside while their engines arrived at Bath in time to be serviced and then head trains back to the Midlands. One interesting train which ran 1960-2 was a Cleethorpes to Sidmouth and Exmouth train, the coaching stock being Eastern Region and Southern Region operated on alternate Saturdays. All through expresses were withdrawn from the route on 10th September, 1962.

Bath Green Park enamel sign as displayed on lamp posts.   *Author*

At Newton Meadows class '5' No. 44815 works the 10-coach down 'Pines Express' on 22nd March, 1952.   *R.E. Toop*

Class '4F' class 0-6-0 No. 43926 (22A, Bristol) at Weston, heads a St John's/Emmanuel Sunday School special bound for Weston-super-Mare on 26th June, 1954. Weston station, had to be reopened specially, having closed to passengers on 21st September, 1953.   *F. Basil Robbins*

Class '2P' 4-4-0 No. 40563 and class '7F' 2-8-0 No. 53801 head a train of ex-LNER coaches from Cleethorpes to Exmouth, seen at Bath on 16th July, 1960. The first coach is beyond the platform. Ex-GWR '57XX' class 0-6-0PT No. 3742 stands on the bridge. *Colin Roberts*

'Jubilee' class '6P' 4-6-0 No. 45639 *Raleigh* (55A, Leeds) at Bath Junction with the 7.45 am Bradford Forster Square to Bournemouth West, 8th September, 1962. Notice the sludge tender to the right of the engine's smokebox. A gas holder is on the far right. *E. Wilmshurst*

Push-pull working

These trains were hard work for a fireman and it was not unknown for them to take food back home at the end of a shift simply because they had had no time to eat it - all the station time being used for taking on water, unless this was carried out by a kindly driver who allowed a break. It was not until the service had been worked for some time that it was realised that firemen on these workings should be 'Passed' (i.e. passed for driving), not Registered Firemen, and certainly not Passed Cleaners, it not being safe for an inexperienced man to be alone on the footplate.

The three push-and-pull coaches were stabled on the bridge at Bath. The locomotive left the shed bunker-first and coupled to the coaches, the engine at the Bath end of the train. The two vacuum pipes had different pattern ends so that it was impossible to couple the vacuum brake pipe to the vacuum regulator pipe. A double cylinder on the smoke box cut steam off, or applied it. The fireman, apart from looking after fire and water, was required to operate the cut-off and open the regulator initially. He also had to turn on the blower when his driver shut the regulator. Electric bell communication was provided between the driver's vestibule and engine cab.

One driver let his mate fire and drive the engine, the driver giving all his attention to operating the brake, observing signals and the lady guard. A problem experienced when pushing a train on a cold morning was that steam leaking from the heating hose at the leading end of the train, tended to douse the headlamp. If possible, an SR headlamp was used as this pattern seemed less prone to trouble.

After stopping at Yate, the train ran to Wickwar to cross over to the down road and at Mangotsfield stopped for water. The fire was cleaned at Barrow Road motive power depot. 0-4-4T No. 1348 was popular for working push-pulls as it had four coal rails rather than three, consequently coal could be stacked higher - a decided advantage as it worked about 80 miles in the morning and 70 in the afternoon.

Bath footplatemen were sent to the Nailsworth branch for instruction on push-pull trains prior to their introduction on the Mangotsfield line. Here we see a Stonehouse-Stroud train in September 1937 pushed by Class '1P' 0-4-4T No. 1390.   *P. Strange*

Chapter Ten

Goods Train Services and Operation

Goods services

In January 1870 one goods train ran from Bristol to Weston which dealt with Bath traffic until the facilities at the latter place were finished; one train ran from Weston to Mangotsfield. In June, following the opening of the Bath goods sheds trains were as follows: two from Bath to Mangotsfield; one Bath to St Philip's; three Mangotsfield to Bath and one St Philip's to Bath. By May 1914 goods and mail services had vastly increased, trains being run to Bath from Bristol (6); Gloucester (3); Birmingham (2); Westerleigh (1); Avonmouth Docks (1); and one from Mangotsfield carrying fish. On Sundays there were two trains from Bristol, one from Sharpness, two from Birmingham and one from Gloucester. From Bath goods trains ran to Westerleigh (5); Bristol (3); Gloucester (2); Avonmouth (2); Sharpness (1 Sundays-only); and Birmingham (1).

The freight timetable for the summer of 1939 showed through goods or minerals from Fishponds, Westerleigh, Bristol, Birmingham, Avonmouth and Weston. None ran on Sundays. In the other direction they ran from Bath to Westerleigh, Bristol, Weston, Gloucester, Avonmouth and Birmingham. There were Sunday trains to Westerleigh and Bristol. During the season fruit specials ran from the Tamar Valley and Swanwick (both originating on the Southern Railway) to Derby. They left Bath at 9.20 pm and 9.50 pm respectively, and on the days when these specials ran, the normal 9.15 pm to Birmingham departed at 9.05.

In September 1953 the first goods train to leave Bath was the 12.20 am empties from Midland Bridge Road to Washwood Heath, followed by the 2.44 am to Westerleigh; 4.00 empties to Washwood Heath; 4.35 to Westerleigh; 5.30 to Warmley; 7.00 to Bristol; 9.23 to Westerleigh; 10.45 empties to Washwood Heath; 1.00 pm to Westerleigh; 2.10 pick-up freight to Westerleigh; 8.20 to Avonmouth; 9.15 to Water Orton; 10.30 to Bristol and the 11.29 to Westerleigh. On Sundays there was the 12.20 am empties to Washwood Heath and the 2.45 am to Westerleigh.

The first train to arrive at Bath Midland Bridge Road was the 11.10 pm from Avonmouth at 1.00 am; the 1.02 am Westerleigh Sidings which arrived Midland Bridge Road 1.56; 4.55 am saw the arrival of the 10.35 pm ex-Kings Norton; at 6.30 the train which had left Bath at 5.30 am to shunt at Warmley returned; the 6.52 from Westerleigh arrived at 8.35 and on Mondays only the 2.30 am from Kings Norton arrived at 8.45. The 10.55 am ex-Westerleigh arrived at 11.32 and the 11.35 from the same place at 12.15 pm. The 7.15 am from Washwood Heath arrived at 2.20 pm and the 2.40 pm from Westerleigh arrived at Bath Junction at 3.25. The 6.10 pm from Bristol arrived at 7.5, and finally the 6.30 from Westerleigh at 7.27. On Sundays the 12.50 am from Westerleigh arrived Bath Junction at 1.46 am.

MR dray at Carr's Mill, Twerton *c.*1910.   *Author's Collection*

USED IN ROYAL HOUSEHOLDS.

A CONSIGNMENT OF

HUNDREDS OF TESTIMONIALS

CHIVERS' CARPET SOAP

WHICH IS SENT TO ALL PARTS OF THE WORLD.

SOLE MANUFACTURERS F. CHIVERS & CO., SOAP WORKS, BATH, ENG.

Chivers' carpet soap *en route* on MR drays from the factory at Twerton to the Midland Bridge goods yard. This trade card dates from *c.*1910. *M.J. Tozer Collection*

Freight timetable 7th September, 1964 to 13th June, 1965

Turn 955:	(2-8-0 '8F') 6.27 am depart from Midland Bridge Road to Westerleigh, St Philip's, Kingswood, Avonmouth, arriving at Bath S&D Yard 12.05 pm. Depart Midland Bridge Road 6.27 pm to Westerleigh arriving back at S&D Yard 8.55 pm.
Turn 956:	(2-8-0 '8F') Depart Midland Bridge Road 4.40 am to Ashton Sidings, run light engine to Westerleigh and take train to Bath, arriving S&D Yard 8.45. Leave at 9.15 am shunting Weston and Brewery Sidings if required, shunting at Bitton and arriving back at S&D Yard 10.40 am.
Turn 962:	2,500 hp Sulzer diesel electric off the 11.49 am Bristol passenger. Depart Midland Bridge Road 1.00 pm to Westerleigh, arrive S&D Yard 3.45.
Turn 964:	(0-6-0 '4F') Depart Midland Bridge Road 5.30 am, shunt at Warmley, Westerleigh, Stapleton Road Gas Works, Fishponds, Westerleigh, Stapleton Road Gas Works, arriving Bath S&D Yard 1.02 pm.
Turn 965:	(0-6-0 '4F') Midland Bridge Road depart 11.29 pm to Westerleigh, arrive at S&D Yard 1.45 am; 2.30 am depart for Westerleigh, arrive back at 4.57 am to shed, then shunt the 12.37 am Leicester parcels.
Turn 966:	(ex-GWR '5700' 0-6-0PT) Shunt 2.10 am-8.20 am; 2.00 pm-6.00 pm.
Turn 969:	(ex-GWR '5700' 0-6-0PT) Shunt 6.30 am-9.10 pm.
Turn 971:	('82XXX', 2-6-2T '3MT') Green Park passenger shunting 5.05 pm-6.05 pm and 8.10 pm-10.15 pm.

Weston Brewery siding on 16th June, 1945. The shunting capstans can be seen each side of the right-hand siding and the rope incorrectly draped across the nearest road. These sidings were taken out of use on 5th May, 1968.

Author's Collection

A farm train at Bitton in September 1933. One wagon is carrying implements and in front of the cattle wagon on the left is a container loaded with farm house furniture. The goods shed is on the left and notice that the end of the passenger station building carries an advertisement for Lux soap flakes. *Bath Evening Chronicle*

Bath goods shed from the north on 20th December, 1967, following the lifting of track to Green Park station. *Author*

View up towards Bath Junction in February 1967 following track lifting. *C. Steane*

Bath Midland Bridge Road goods shed, yard and sidings, February 1967. *C. Steane*

'4F' class 0-6-0 No. 4166 approaches Weston with the up midday freight on 21st June, 1936. The gantry in the left background is for the renewal of Locksbrook Bridge. The upper quadrant signals are newly-erected.   *Revd Alan Newman*

Class '4F' 0-6-0 No. 44096 has steam to spare climbing the 1 in 121 through Bitton on 6th May, 1954, with an up train mostly comprising empty wagons.   *C. Gordon Watford*

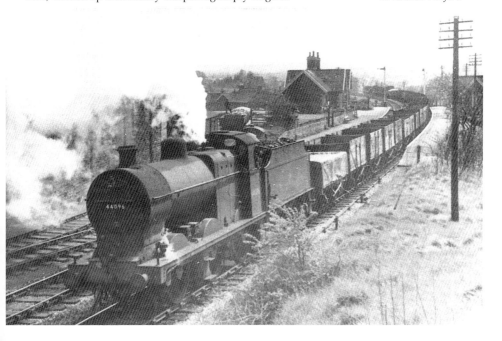

A very rare visitor: Fowler class '4P' 2-6-4T No. 42338 passes Weston Brewery with a down permanent way train, 19th August, 1955. The sidings are beyond the fence on the left. *Author*

Ex-S&D class '3F' 0-6-0 No. 43201 with the 2.10 pm pick-up freight at Newbridge, Bath, 22nd August, 1955. *Author*

Westerleigh Yard closed on 22nd February, 1965, after which freights worked to and from Stoke Gifford.

Freight timetable 7th September, 1965 to 17th April, 1966

Turn 954:   2-8-0 '8F' to work the 11.45 am Bath Midland Bridge Road to Portishead arriving back at Midland Bridge Road 4.42 pm, 9.25 pm Midland Bridge Road to Stoke Gifford, returning at 12.55 am and arriving Bath 2.57 am. 3.25 pm Midland Bridge Road to Stoke Gifford arrive Bath 8.00 pm.

Turn 955:   3.15 am Bath S&D Yard for Bristol West Depot, arriving back at 7.35 am. Depart 7.50 am to shunt Weston and Brewery Sidings if required, returning to S&D Yard 8.20 am.

Turn 956:   4.40 am Midland Bridge Road to Ashton Junction, Bristol East Depot, Kingsland Road, Pylle Hill and Bristol West Depot. Return light engine to Bath shed arriving 11 am.

During the same period there were two shunting engines at Bath: one worked 72 hours 40 minutes a week shunting the goods yard and banking up the S&D to Combe Down tunnel, while the other worked 12½ hours a week shunting the S&D Yard and locomotive sidings.

Goods working

An interesting train was the 2.10 pm 'Warmley Shunt', an engine and van which shunted Jobbins' coal yard at Weston, then Long's timber siding and Weston Brewery. It shunted at Bitton, mostly coal wagons being dropped off, though there were often a few box vans for the goods shed. Sometimes in the 1940s it had 45 vehicles when leaving Bitton, in which case it ran through to Westerleigh, returning to shunt at Warmley where there was usually about an hour's work. Once a fireman on the 2.10 had severe toothache. At Warmley he asked the whereabouts of the nearest dentist and was told Kingswood, over a mile distant. While the driver attended to the fire and shunted, the fireman caught a bus, had his offending tooth extracted under gas, returned by bus to Warmley and carried on firing to Westerleigh! He remembers that day in August 1953 vividly as Denis Compton was batting, made the decisive run, and England won the Ashes. The 'Warmley Shunt' left Warmley at about 6 pm for Westerleigh and returned each evening with up to 40 trucks of beer, some travelling via the SR and destined for the Royal Navy at Devonport.

In the 1950s the 6.27 pm goods took coal to Westerleigh, shunted, then crossed to the down side to work the 7.08 pm thence to St Philip's Yard. After uncoupling from the train, it pushed the brake van up to Kingswood Junction and ran to Avonmouth, working a heavy goods back - 16 or 18 wagons of animal feed bound for the Blandford warehouse. Usually the engine was a '4F' 0-6-0. No banker was provided and if the distant signal at Sea Mills was off, the regulator was opened to get a run at this gradient. A full boiler of steam and a full box of fire was essential. If the engine stalled in Clifton Down tunnel, the signalman was contacted by phone and the train divided. Sometimes a banana special was arranged to run from Avonmouth to Bath. If there were more than

The 2.10 pm Bath to Westerleigh pick-up goods: ex-S&D class '7F' 2-8-0 No. 53802 with an ex-GWR brake van at Newbridge, Bath, 6th April, 1956.   *Author*

Ex-S&D class '7F' 2-8-0 No. 53806 comes through Warmley with a lengthy goods train on 27th July, 1963. About half the train consists of coal wagons destined for Bath Gas Works.
R.E. Toop

Ex-S&D class '7F' 2-8-0 No. 53800 passes the site of Kelston station, 5th May, 1956. *R.E. Toop*

Class '8F' 2-8-0 No. 48737 (82F, Bath), with an up evening goods train below Kelston Park on 16th June, 1964, gets up speed to tackle Bitton Bank. *Author*

The Midland Bridge Road goods shed from the cab of diesel-hydraulic type '1' 0-6-0 No. D9521, April 1966.   *Author's Collection*

'Hymek' No. D7025 near Bath gas works, 3rd February, 1968.   *Colin Roberts Collection*

18 vans, a class '7F' 2-8-0 left the first 18 at Fishponds and returned to Avonmouth for the remainder.

On a heavy through up freight from Bath it was common practice for a driver to get a run at Bitton Bank which started at the last bridge across the Avon. Wagons with grease axle boxes ran more freely when loaded than when empty, the weight making the grease warm quicker. On a cold morning, the driver of an up empty wagon train ran fast from Bath to Kelston attempting to warm the boxes prior to ascending Bitton Bank. He had to beware of going too fast, or the grease would overheat, ignite and that wagon have to be put off.

Coal from Norton Hill Colliery, Midsomer Norton, was taken to Westerleigh, a 'tripper' then working it to Portishead, though later practice was for Bath men to take it to Ashton Meadows. If a class '4F' 0-6-0 had a load of about 46 wagons up Bitton Bank, it was often struggling for steam by the time it reached Bitton signal box. A wise fireman persuaded his driver to stay at Bath until the fire was to his liking; if he failed to do this, he might have to stop at Bitton to 'blow up'.

During World War II a maximum of 58 empty wagons was allowed on the line. This figure could not be exceeded because if a train had more than this number and stopped at Mangotsfield North, the brake van would have fouled the catch point and have been derailed if the train moved back. A guard always had to apply his brakes hard when near catch points to avoid being pushed backwards off the road by expanding buffers. Latterly this risk was obviated by rodding linking the motor points at the South Junction with the catch points in the North Curve.

On a Westerleigh trip the engine had to return tender first as no turntable was provided at the yard. The first thing a driver did when he booked on to work a Westerleigh freight was to look for a storm sheet to give some protection when working back to Bath. A driver kept such a sheet in his locker. His locker also held his black lodging box with working timetables and addenda stored in the lid and food in the box itself, together with a hand lamp; flare lamp used for oiling and known as a 'gawky'; and a dirty coat for protecting his overalls when oiling. Some men had two or three lockers for their belongings acquired by appropriating one from someone who had left. Conversely some cleaners could not get a locker because 'they were all taken'.

Working tender first a fireman tried to place sufficient coal in the box to avoid the need to fire on the move, for shovelling coal raised dust which blew back on the crew. On the up journey he watered the coal as much as possible to soak it thoroughly; nevertheless pockets of dry, dusty coal remained under lumps. If proceeding tender first on a cold night, it was common practice to leave the firehole door open to help keep you warm, though this was not possible during the war because it infringed blackout regulations.

The Midland's policy of avoiding facing crossovers wherever possible was observed at Bath. A down freight stopped approximately by the Engine Shed Junction, backed on to the up line by Bath Junction signal box and then drew forward on to the goods reception line, the engine being uncoupled and run to the shed while the shunter emerged from the spur, buffered up to the brake van and commenced shunting. A freight off the S&D could run straight on to the reception line.

Bath Junction signal box - view towards Green Park station *c.1966*. The Mangotsfield line was on the far side of the box.   *C. Steane*

Warmley signal box, now a listed building, 23rd August, 1988.   *Author*

Chapter Eleven

Signalling, Permanent Way and Accidents

Signalling

Signal boxes were classified on the number of lever movements - the more movements, the higher the class (i.e. the lower the classification number). Boxes on the line were classified as follows:

Bath Station Class 2
Bath Junction Class 3 (became Class 2 in the 1950s)
    (For comparison, the former GWR boxes at Bath Station and Bath Goods were only Class 3)
Weston Class 3 (Prior to 1949, Class 4)
Bitton Class 4 (Closed at night and on Sundays) (Prior to 1949, Class 5)
Warmley Class 3 (Prior to 1949, Class 4)
Mangotsfield North Class 3
Mangotsfield Station Class 2

The 41-lever Bath Station box was double-manned on summer Saturdays from 6 am until 10 pm, one signalman working the levers, while the other was in telephone communication with Control and Bath Junction. A tablet dropped on a summer Saturday from an up S&D train put everything out, because apart from delaying that train and those following, down trains from the Midlands were also delayed as the incoming engines off up S&D trains, due to take them forward, were late. The delay could hold trains 'block to block' from Mangotsfield to Bath.

Ex-GWR men could not understand some of the signalling at Green Park. The centre carriage road on the departure side had a dummy towards the outwards end of the platform. When green it showed access to the main line, but when the points were set for straight ahead, it displayed red and not yellow. If making a shunting movement, an engine was permitted to go past it at red, but the GWR could not accept that it was in order to pass a red signal, unless in permissive block working. The three ground frames at Bath station: Carriage Siding, Arrival Line and Departure Line, were unlocked from Bath Station signal box by a plunger being pressed in the ground frame requesting the release lever (known as the 'Asking Lever') to be pulled in the signal box. There was a 2 ft diameter brass warning bell near the Bonded Store. The signalman at the Station box rang it using a lever in his box, giving two rings for an incoming Midland train and three for one off the Somerset & Dorset. Carriage shunters polished the bell in their spare time. It is thought that it was removed pre-World War II.

A Bath Junction signalman on a summer Saturday sometimes had no time to eat his lunch. Even when the train service eased, Bath Loco had to sort out engines; this involved sending them out on to the main line. In winter the signalmen at Bath Junction found that they tended to catch bronchitis through going so often from a warm box to the cold outside. They were required to go out three times for just one down S&D freight - to give the engine tablet; then

Weston signal box *c.*1914. Notice the absence of a ramp to the walkway over the point rodding and signal wires, and no fire buckets. Old-pattern insulators are on the telegraph poles. 'Weston' is on the front of the box. Near the foot of the steps, a light (probably orange in colour), turned in conjunction with the crossing gates to indicate their position. This was necessary because the curve prevented a driver from seeing them until he was almost upon them. This lamp was later replaced by a home signal.

M.J. Tozer Collection

the banking key; then to collect the key from the returning banker. Hopmead ground frame was released by the Junction box in a similar manner as the three at Bath station. If a platform was clear to the stop blocks, Bath Station box accepted a train from the Junction and the distant signal was pulled off. Weston's down distant could not be pulled off unless the Junction and Station distants were clear. This meant that usually the Weston distant was only pulled off for an express. The Western Region, staffed mainly by ex-GWR men, objected to this practice of having a green right up to the blocks, but it speeded traffic as a driver knew he had a clear road. Bath Junction box was switched out on Sundays unless any traffic was running over the S&D, but two Sunday turns were worked at Bath Station box, Weston and Warmley.

Eight to ten levers were put in at Bath Junction for single line working, when the bridge between it and Weston was renewed. This addition was virtually an extra signal box. When the bridge works were complete and double line working restored, the levers were left as spare. Bath Junction and Bath Station boxes both closed on 12th September, 1966.

A mercury-operated treadle was situated before Weston's down distant signal. This buzzed when depressed by a train. A signalman had to close the gates before the down 'Pines Express' reached this treadle, because at the speed it normally travelled, there was no time to close the gates and pull off the distant before it reached the latter. The gates were closed to road traffic 2-2½ minutes after receiving 'on line' from Bitton. With a down goods the signalman had more time and did not need to close the gates to road traffic immediately, but waited until the buzzer sounded. The wicket gates were locked at the discretion of the signalman, usually he closed them when a down train was opposite Long's siding. Each wicket gate was closed by a separate lever. Sometimes a person would hold the gate open for a friend, but the lever would have to be pulled and the gate was snatched from their hand. One man tried to hold the gate open with the front wheel of his bicycle. Because the train was so near, the signalman had to pull the lever, which buckled the wheel. When an up express was put 'on line' by Bath Junction, the wicket gates were closed immediately. Wicket gates similarly operated were installed at Warmley.

Timber Mill ground frame was released from Weston signal box. As the Brewery Siding ground frame was in advance of the up main starter and therefore, 'in section', the ground frame was provided with a distant signal below the home at the west end of Weston's up platform. If the advance starter at Weston was not clear, the ground frame's distant could not be pulled off. The ground frame's home signal was on the up side of the overbridge. In the 1950s the frame was unlocked from Weston signal box by a release lever, this allowing the distant applicable to the ground frame to be abolished. When a train was to shunt at Brewery Sidings, and would therefore arrive at Bitton later than normal, Weston asked Bitton for 'Line Clear' by giving 2-2-3 signifying a train stopping in the section. For a train using Mangotsfield North Curve, Weston sent Bitton 2-2-4 as 'Train Entering Section'.

Weston and Warmley boxes closed on 5th May, 1968, train crews subsequently having to operate the crossing gates. Weston's down distant was replaced by a 'fixed at caution' signal on this date, the arm being attached the wrong way round, but corrected within a few days. Warmley box remained in use as a ground frame. An MR type '4d', it was built in 1918, and still remains on its original site.

Bitton signal box in 1946. *Revd John Fenning*

View of Mangotsfield station from the cab of class '5' 2-6-0 No. 2900 working a train from Bristol to Bath. *W.F. Grainger*

Kelston signal box was only opened between 10 am and 6 pm on summer Saturdays to shorten the 5½ mile-long Bitton to Weston block section, it being first brought into use on 30th May, 1936. The density of traffic was so great that on at least one Saturday before World War II, a train was held at every down signal between Mangotsfield and Bath. Closed for the duration of the war, Kelston box re-opened at least once afterwards, but was closed permanently in 1949. The 4-lever turn-over frame was outside the box, the lamp indicators facing out through the window, though the signals were allowed to remain unlighted during the period the box was closed. The block instruments were inside the small wooden hut situated at the Bath end of the station building on the down platform. There were but four signals: a home and distant for each direction, the up distant on a concrete post - very rare in this district.

Bitton signal box closed on 19th July, 1965 as the goods yard had shut a fortnight before and the train service was not of sufficient intensity to be delayed by a 7½ mile-long section between Warmley and Weston. The box was removed, but has now been replaced by the Avon Valley Railway with a similar structure from Painswick Road Crossing, Gloucester.

Mangotsfield Station signal box dealt with some trains it never saw except on the track circuit, points at Mangotsfield South Junction being operated by Siemens General Electric 30v electric motors, power coming from a battery trickle-charged from the mains. Bath to Mangotsfield North trains were invisible from the cabin. When an up train passed Warmley up starting signal it was immediately shown on the Mangotsfield Station signal box track circuit 3111; at the distant signals it was on track circuit 3110 and when 200 yds to the rear of the South Junction home signals it went on track circuit 3109. All these circuits were unique in the fact that the track circuit in advance of the train had to be occupied before that to the rear showed clear, thus preventing a train getting 'lost' in the rear section. The only exception to this was if Warmley starting signal was in the 'on' position and a long train was shunting. In the event of it entering track circuit 3111 and then setting back to the rear of Warmley starting signal, track circuit 3111 would clear. On the down road at Mangotsfield South Junction, approaching from the North Junction, a treadle was set in advance of the down home signal to warn the Station signalman that he was to give 'Train Entering Section' to Warmley, although in practice this was usually done when the train passed Mangotsfield North, in order to give the Warmley signalman time to open his crossing gates and give the driver the distant signal.

If a signalman annoyed a driver, it was prudent for him to close his windows before the engine passed, this preventing water from the pet pipe being squirted through.

Unless a driver found the correct signals pulled off, he was required to give the following whistles:

Mangotsfield Station:	Up train from Bristol for Bath - 3
	Up line from Bath to Bristol - 2; Gloucester - 3
Mangotsfield North:	Stopping at Westerleigh Sidings - 3
	Down train to Bath - 1
Yate South Junction:	For Bath - 1
Weston:	Mangotsfield North Junction - 3
Bath Junction:	For Weston - 2

'890' class 2-4-0 No. 104 went through the stop blocks at Bath on Friday 13th February, 1925. It had been in charge of a parcels train which arrived at 6.10 am. Notice 'Bath' on the seat back.

Bath Evening Chronicle

S&D 2-8-0 No. 89 ran away and overturned at the entrance to Bath goods yards, 20th November, 1929. The yard inspector inside the demolished cabin was killed.

Author's Collection

Permanent Way

The district permanent way headquarters were at Fishponds. In 1945 permanent way gangs responsible for the branch were:

Bath to just east of Weston
Weston to below Kelston Park
Kelston Park to Bitton
Bitton to Mangotsfield
Mangotsfield gang

The first gang had eight men, the other gangs about four men each. Duties were varied: the ganger crouched down and looked along the rail to find undulations in the track which were then corrected; fishplates and points required oiling; drains needed cleaning to keep the ballast dry; the ballast on the main line had to be sieved - this was tiring. Although the main line was kept clean by the weed killing train, it did not cover the sidings so these had to be cleaned manually. A pick and shovel were used to loosen weeds which were placed in a bucket and thrown down the bank. The grass on either side of the track required scything, while lineside fences and hedges needed maintenance. Before setting fire to a bank to burn the dried grass, the top required burning in a controlled manner to act as a fire break. One man in the Weston gang, taking less care than he should, set fire to a cherry tree in Rudmore Park adjacent to the railway. The owner succeeded in claiming £14 damages from the railway. A few years later, the tree's owner saw the permanent way men and asked if they would burn it down again because it had made his tree give a heavier crop. A permanent way ganger picked primroses from embankments near Bitton, bunched and took them to Bath on a Saturday. This practice led to him being nicknamed 'Posy Pitt'.

In 1934 a start was made in relaying the branch with 90 lb./yd rail to carry the heaviest LMS engines which could use the line on completion of the bridge rebuilding programme. As far as possible this track relaying was carried out between trains so as to reduce Sunday work to a minimum. The track was kept up-to-date, some flat-bottomed rail being laid in Newton Meadows in 1959, while four years later welded rail appeared on the up line at Kelston.

Accidents

Fortunately the branch has been free of serious accidents involving passengers. On 20th January, 1880 the 9.45 am goods from Bristol was passing Bitton when the signalman noticed sparks coming from the centre of the train and alerted the driver. It was found that a wagon carrying oranges had derailed. Its body was shattered and oranges scattered over the line for some distance. It was believed that an axle had broken shortly after leaving Warmley, for the permanent way was damaged for two miles. Double line working could not be resumed until 3 pm the following day.

As the 9 pm up train neared Kelston on 10th November, 1887, the driver missed his fireman John Knight aged 24. He stopped, and Knight was found lying a short distance to the rear of the train. He was insensible, his head severely cut having evidently come into contact with the wall of the bridge near where he was lying. The driver of the 8.35 pm from Bristol stopped and took the injured man to Bath. At the Royal United Hospital it was found that his skull was fractured in two places and his body bruised. It was thought that Knight, reaching for his pricker, or dart, kept at the side of the engine, overbalanced and fell. He died the following day.

At about 4.30 am on 15th November, 1919 a goods train from Bristol left its rear portion near Weston signal box while the engine shunted Jobbins' siding. While operations were proceeding, a wagon became derailed and before it could be put back on the track, a goods from Gloucester struck the rear portion of the train left west of the station. The impact caused the drawbar of a coal wagon of the standing train to be broken and shot the trucks forward into the wagon already off the road causing rolling stock to pile up over the up and down lines blocking them completely. It was very fortunate that the collision did not occur a few minutes later, as it would then have caused serious injury to W.G. Huntley, the Bath locomotive foreman, and a gang of men getting under the derailed wagon prior to re-railing it. The goods from Gloucester did not escape scot free. The collision derailed the engine which cut through the ballast fracturing a gas main, the supply of which had to be shut off to prevent the escaping gas igniting. The track was not cleared for single line working until 11.30 am.

The mishap which is almost inevitable sometime in the life of a terminal station, occurred on 13th February, 1925. 2-4-0 No. 104 hauling a parcels train from the Midlands and due in at 6.10 am, overran 27 ft demolishing the blocks and an ornamental bank of ferns and mounted the platform. A W.H. Smith & Sons' newsboy sitting on the seat with his back to the buffers, heard furious whistling from the approaching train and moved away. This was fortunate as his seat was shattered and his abandoned overcoat found beneath the engine. Although an S&D breakdown crane was at Bath, this could not be called out as the derailment was not to that company's train, but that of the LMS, a breakdown train having to be summoned from Bristol. The wheels were placed on packing to prevent them sinking through the wooden floor into the bonded store and two engines unsuccessfully attempted to draw No. 104 back on to the track. The wheels were then jacked up and a third engine coupled on and they succeeded in pulling it down to the permanent way at 11.10 am.

The final accident was the most serious and occurred to an S&D train on LMS metals, though the real cause was on S&D territory. On 20th November, 1929 the crew of 2-8-0 No. 89, later LMS No. 13809 (now preserved), hauling the 3.25 pm Evercreech Junction to Bath became overcome by fumes as the locomotive toiled up the 1 in 100 through the 1,829 yards-long single bore Combe Down tunnel, and when the engine and train started the 1 in 50 descent to Bath, no one on the footplate was conscious to apply the brakes. The train sped round the curve by Bath Junction signal box at a speed probably in excess of 50 mph, crashed at the entrance to Bath goods yard, the wagons piling in a great heap. The office cabin was demolished killing the yard inspector inside. Driver Jennings died and another fatality was a young LMS clerk from Gloucester taking a short cut through the yard on his way home from work. He was struck on the head by part of a gas lamp standard.

Chapter Twelve

The Avon Valley Railway
Past, Present and Beyond

On 6th March, 1966, driver Archie Gunning, fireman Albert Parsons and guard Bernard Ware were working the last train over the Somerset & Dorset Railway prior to the cessation of passenger services over that line and the Mangotsfield to Bath Branch. Twenty-five years later to the day, 6th March 1991, those same three gentlemen were guests of honour at a much happier occasion - the opening of the Avon Valley Railway's new line extension from Bitton Station to Oldland Common.

The story of the rebirth of this part of the former branch line goes back to 1972 when a group of local people set up 'The Bristol Suburban Railway Society' based at Bitton station, with the grand aim of re-opening the line for a commuter service. Although the station building had, by now, been reduced to a shell, the society was granted permission to use Bitton as its base and work began to restore the building and re-lay track. In 1974 the first train rides were possible and, although there were only 100 yards of track, the public response was tremendous, encouraging the society to continue with its plans for the future.

In 1979 the Bristol Suburban Railway Society was incorporated into the Bitton Railway Company Ltd, with a new aim of preserving the line in order to operate trains for public benefit and to educate, stimulate and encourage interest in railway preservation. For the next few years work continued in extending the line northwards towards the site of Oldland Halt. Although this was completed in 1988, the track remained unused for a number of years whilst a legal battle was fought by a small number of neighbours opposed to the opening of the railway. The case was eventually won by the railway, but at the cost of over £30,000 in legal and other fees - valuable money which had been intended for use on further expansion.

The increase in line length, although still quite short in comparison with many preserved railways, persuaded many passengers to travel even though, at this stage, they were not able to alight at the other end. By the close of 1991 twice as many people had travelled on the line as in the previous year, with a climax of a record 5,700 passengers in one 'Friends of Thomas the Tank Engine' day! This extra income went some way to paying off the debts incurred in obtaining the Light Railway Order and eventually a new platform, complete with a run-round loop, was built at Oldland Common and opened in 1999.

In the meantime, further expansion northwards had become impractical due to developments in local transport and housing. Consequently, the Railway decided to concentrate on a southern extension and work began on raising money to purchase track for the push towards the River Avon and Bath.

Work on laying the track southwards began in 1992, giving both volunteers and the public their first taste of the scenic Avon Valley. However, with rail and sleepers costing some £75,000 per mile to buy and the cost of the Public Enquiry still blighting the Railway's finances, progress was slow. By this time local

The exterior of Bitton station on 11th January, 1989 with an LMS dray in the forecourt. *Author*

Bitton station on 8th May, 1976 with ex-BR coach No. 15447, *right*.   *Author*

0-6-0ST *Edwin Hulse* built by Avonside, No. 1798 of 1918, receiving attention at Bitton on 8th May, 1976. *Author*

Harlech Television's 'Telethon Special' headed by 0-6-0ST *Fonmon*, built by Peckett, No. 1636 in 1929, approaching Bitton on 30th May, 1988. (Telethon was an ITV fund-raising scheme.)
Author

Class '8F' 2-8-0 No. 48173 undergoing restoration at Bitton on 11th January, 1989. Its Fowler
tender came from class '4F' 0-6-0 No. 44422.   *Author*

Class '1F' 0-6-0T No. 41708 arrives at Bitton on 3rd May, 1999.   *Author*

authority boundary changes meant that the Railway, including the line south to the river, had come into the new county of South Gloucestershire. Over several months a good relationship was forged with the council, acknowledging the potential which the Railway provided for leisure access to the river valley. As with the original railway pioneers, the considerable hurdles placed in the way of the volunteers were dealt with one by one and, as the 21st century approached, the line was extended to within a stone's throw of the first major crossing of the River Avon.

The River Avon Project

The large-scale project of 2000-2004, which cost the Avon Valley Railway £150,000, was the extension of the line southwards for around 400 metres. Although only covering a short distance, the extension required track to be relaid across the river bridge (involving a highly expensive safety examination of the structure), plus the construction of a brand new platform with a run-round loop.

The all-important Parliamentary Transport & Works Order was granted, as was planning permission by both South Gloucestershire Council and Bath & North East Somerset Council. The fact that the boundary between the two counties met in the centre of the River Avon bridge made for interesting negotiations. Funding for the project came from a number of sources, including railway revenue and grants from local schemes such as the Churngold Environmental Fund.

Before any work could begin on laying track or building a platform, the railway was required to 'divert' the Bristol and Bath Railway Path, a walking and cycling route between Bristol and Bath using one half of the former trackbed, to one side of the narrow cutting to provide sufficient room. Using mainly volunteer labour, this work took almost 12 months and over £25,000 to complete. The building of the platform and associated track work, although complex and requiring large quantities of materials to be delivered by rail to the site, was completed in just over a year. However, unlike the earlier construction of the Oldland platform, powering the lights at the station posed something of a problem as the nearest electricity supply was half a mile away. The solution came in the form of a portable generator to be conveyed to the site, when required, on the first train of the day.

The construction of the new platform, known as 'Avon Riverside', marked a watershed moment in the life of the revived line. Trains no longer required 'top-and-tail' engines on the southbound journey and spectators can watch steam engines running round and coupling up at both ends of the line. Amongst other advantages, it enables passengers and users of the Bristol and Bath Railway Path - including the disabled - to reach the riverside and picnic area. British Waterways have added to the facilities by building a 50 metre landing stage at the river bank, allowing craft using the river to tie up alongside. Within walking distance there are several excellent pubs while the large and popular Avon Valley Country Park is close by.

The end of the line, view east on 18th January, 1997 preparatory to the extension to Avon Riverside. *Author*

A new charity, 'The Avon Valley Railway Heritage Trust', was established to preserve the railway heritage of the area and to operate trains for educational and instructional purposes. Meanwhile, at Bitton work continues on the buildings and site. Decorative barge boards, a distinctive feature of the original station building, have been fitted to the eaves at the front of the building. Boards such as these originally decorated all five eaves and it is planned that eventually all will be replaced. In the station yard the original 1860s goods shed, currently the railway's workshop, has been totally re-roofed and is the only covered accommodation where restoration work can be carried out.

As with any preserved railway, there is always restoration work taking place on locomotives, carriages and wagons - all carried out by volunteers.

Future plans

With the completion of the Avon Riverside project, money continues to be raised in order to fund ambitious plans for Bitton station itself. It is intended that new facilities will include a new locomotive and carriage restoration shed complete with a viewing area, enabling visitors to see work in progress. There are also plans for a museum and educational facilities, plus improved catering and toilet accommodation. The long term plan is to extend the line to the outskirts of Bath and a site has already been identified as a possible southern terminus. This would offer a return trip of some 14 miles through the scenic countryside of the Avon Valley.

The Avon Valley Railway, now a major tourist attraction receiving up to 80,000 visitors a year, is already showing the potential to become the catalyst that brings together a whole range of attractions in the area. As the railway develops, visitors will be able to use its trains to explore more of the Avon valley and the delights which, for many people, have been hidden from view.

Avon Valley Railway Stock List

Locomotives

Name	No.	Origin	Class	Type	Built	Notes
	41708	MR	1F	0-6-0T	1880	Under restoration away from Bitton
Sir Frederick Pile	34058	SR	BB	4-6-2	1947	Under restoration at Bitton
	44123	LMS	4F	0-6-0	1925	Under restoration at Bitton
	48173	LMS	8F	2-8-0	1943	Under restoration at Bitton
	D2994	BR	07	0-6-0DE	1962	In use at Bitton

Avon Valley Railway Stock List (continued)

Diesel Multiple Units

No.	Origin	Class	Type	Built	Notes
51909	BR	108	DMBS	1960	In store at Long Marston
56271	BR	108	DTC	1959	In store at Long Marston

Industrial Locomotives

Name	No.	Builder	Works No.	Type	Built	Notes
	7151	Robert Stephenson & Hawthorns	7151	0-6-0T	1944	In use at Bitton
Littleton No. 5		Manning, Wardle	2018	0-6-0ST	1922	Awaiting restoration at Bitton
Meteor	1	Robert Stephenson & Hawthorns	7609	0-6-0T	1950	Under restoration at Bitton
Edwin Hulse		Avonside	1798	0-6-0ST	1918	Under restoration at Bitton
Karel	4015	Chrzanow	4015	0-6-0T	1954	In use at Bitton
Grumpy	WD70031	Drewry	2158	0-4-0DM	1941	Stored at Bitton
General Lord Robertson	610	Sentinel	10143	0-8-0DH	1963	In use at Bitton
Kingswood		Barclay	446	0-4-0DM	1959	In use at Bitton
Phoenix	70	Hudswell, Clarke	1464	0-6-0T	1921	In use at Bitton
	Army 200	Barclay	358	0-4-0DM	1941	In store at Long Marston
Basil		Ruston & Hornsby	235519	4wDM	1945	Under restoration at Long Marston
		Ruston & Hornsby	252823	4wDM	1947	Chassis only at Bitton
		Ruston & Hornsby	210481	4wDM	1941	Chassis only at Long Marston
Western Pride	D1171	Hudswell, Clarke	D1171	0-6-0DM	1951	In store at Long Marston
	PWM3769	Wickham	6648	2w-2PMR	1953	In use at Bitton

Carriages

No.	Other No.	Type	Built	Notes
1867	977752	RMB	1961	Under restoration away from Bitton
1933		RUB	1959	In use - Steam'n'Cuisine set at Bitton (named Doris)
2599		SLSTP	1959	Dormitory coach for members at Bitton
3051	DB977492	FO	1954	Awaiting restoration at Long Marston
3089	DB977351	FO	1959	Awaiting restoration at Long Marston
3745		TSO	1953	In use at Bitton (named 'Ruth')
3746		TSO	1953	Awaiting restoration at Long Marston
3749		TSO	1953	Awaiting restoration at Long Marston
3815	AD3305	TSO	1953	Awaiting restoration at Bitton
3991	DB977627	TSO	1954	Awaiting restoration at Long Marston
4035		TSO	1956	Seating for Buffet/Bitton Bears coach at Bitton
4058		TSO	1956	Awaiting restoration at Long Marston
4754	WGP 8806	TSO	1957	In use - Steam'n'Cuisine set at Bitton (named Bicester Military Railway)
6839	DS70244	BCK	1935	Awaiting restoration at Bitton
9208	DB977134	BSO	1955	In use - Steam'n'Cuisine set at Bitton (named Grace)
13231	DB977132	FK	1959	In use - Steam'n'Cuisine set at Bitton (named Martha)
14031		BFK	1966	Awaiting restoration at Long Marston
25040		SK	1956	In use at Bitton
25299		SK	1957	In use at Bitton
25735	DB977635	SK	1961	Awaiting restoration at Long Marston
25972	99629	SK	1962	Awaiting restoration at Long Marston
34111	AD5318	BSK	1951	Workshop/bookshop/exhibition and sales area at Bitton
34531	DB977410	BSK	1955	Awaiting restoration at Long Marston
35174	AD5319	BSK	1958	Destroyed by fire - vandalism/arson at Bitton
35255		BSK	1958	In use at Bitton
35481	99153	BSK	1962	In use as Mess Coach at Bitton

Also on site: CCT 94438, PMV 1162, PMV 1698, PMV 1712, CCT 2213, 'Fruit D' 92095.

Appendix One

Mangotsfield to Bath Station Statistics 1872 to 1922

Station	Year	No. of passengers booked	Passenger receipts (£)	Parcels, Horses, Dogs Carriages (£)	Total Coaching receipts (£)	Goods Debit	No. of Livestock trucks in and out	Coal, Coke Limestone in and out	Carted tons in and out	Not carted in and out	Minerals in and out	Transhipment (tons)	Station Expenses (£)
Mangotsfield	1872	34,053	1,555	59	1,614	-	61	1917	208	1,417	1,453	83	1,265
	1882	39,452	1,976	276	2,252	-	76	142,738	409	5,837	11,816	-	1,721
	1892	43,061	2,019	260	2,279	-	78	113,078	267	6,447	14,665	-	1,809
	1902	37,410	2,137	381	2,518	1,069	79	123,457	270	4,455	10,724	-	2,778
	1912	31,491	1,965	214	2,179	2,703	105	132,411	606	5,575	23,106	-	2,814
	1922	29,931	3,581	397	3,978	8,241	165	84,381	2,165	2,040	8,987	-	7,263
Warmley	1872	32,435	1,030	48	1,098	-	13	3,027	366	945	282	-	201
	1882	30,886	1,085	46	1,131	-	67	7,168	609	2,203	3,344	-	255
	1892	40,095 (57)	1,429	141	1,570	-	277	5,168	5,458	3,850	8,573	-	749
	1902	33,637 (87)	1,289	367	1,656	5,312	148	7,963	8,499	6,665	6,296	-	1,281
	1912	31,127 (97)	1,314	260	1,574	7,726	236	11,157	8,157	5,594	19,016	-	1,491
	1922	29,907 (116)	1,856	2,981	4,837	20,229	544	15,677	5,916	7,919	12,885	-	3,944
Bitton	1872	32,033	1,213	76	1,289	-	3	2,289	2,045	2,800	1,064	-	241
	1882	36,414	1,306	129	1,435	-	60	9,233	686	5,499	427	-	289
	1892	38,887 (74)	1,513	205	1,718	-	42	1,576	701	3,469	430	-	295
	1902	35,450 (85)	1,293	459	1,752	3,273	83	6,953	1,298	4,892	2,829	-	369
	1912	35,322 (157)	1,663	274	1,937	4,051	115	13,421	1,357	4,794	5,106	-	445
	1922	29,998 (156)	2,262	446	2,708	8,422	87	5,675	1,874	3,851	1,086	-	1,167
Kelston	1872	14,464	314	9	323	-	-	-	-	-	-	-	73
	1882	12,841	379	28	407	-	-	-	-	-	-	-	50
	1892	13,702 (16)	398	20	418	-	-	-	-	-	-	-	52
	1902	12,846 (17)	353	14	367	-	-	-	-	-	-	-	70
	1912	8,811 (10)	261	14	275	-	-	-	-	-	-	-	65
	1922	10,288 (26)	477	24	501	-	-	-	-	-	-	-	314
Weston	1872	29,879	699	47	746	-	-	1,398	112	1,567	1,429	-	201
	1882	43,712	879	41	920	-	-	1,517	91	938	1,529	-	292
	1892	56,244 (26)	1,066	93	1,159	-	-	2,220	131	1,885	4,521	-	283
	1902	66,235 (58)	1,063	210	1,273	1,138	-	4,189	82	2,600	2,468	-	347
	1912	11,305 (11)	444	107	551	819	-	2,990	70	1,820	1,880	-	426
	1922	10,025 (38)	955	134	1,089	1,865	-	2,920	243	3,339	1,463	-	1,029

Station	Year	No. of passengers booked	Passenger receipts (£)	Parcels, Horses, Dogs Carriages (£)	Total Coaching receipts (£)	Goods Debit	No. of Livestock trucks in and out	Coal, Coke Limestone in and out	Carted tons in and out	Not carted in and out	Minerals in and out	Tranship-ment (tons)	Station Expenses (£)
Bath (Passenger)	1872	109,282	14,451	3,064	17,515	-	-	-	-	-	-	-	†
	1882	119,449	15,145	3,422	18,567	-	-	-	-	-	-	-	1,693
	1892	117,478 (18)	14,395	4,185	18,580	-	-	-	-	-	-	-	2,023
	1902	90,027 (23)	12,997	5,643	18,640	-	-	-	-	-	-	-	2,352
	1912	57,582 (39)	13,227	5,339	18,566	-	-	-	-	-	-	-	3,023
	1922	50,327 (81)	21,551	5,095	26,646	-	-	-	-	-	-	-	7,383
Bath (Goods)	1872	-	-	-	-	-	451	35,743	8,138	9,576	21,295	104	2,167
	1882	-	-	-	-	-	418	78,593	13,577	26,998	12,544	2,473	4,165
	1892	-	-	-	-	-	1,460	101,178	18,531	27,273	14,799	1,533	4,346
	1902	-	-	-	-	27,032	1,222	112,286	21,819	41,095	21,061	1,739	5,316
	1912	-	-	-	-	23,727	935	137,932	20,665	31,408	31,996	1,406	5,348
	1922	-	-	-	-	35,278	483	147,520	12,745	19,529	24,739	2,525	9,032

Number shown in brackets indicate number of season tickets sold.
† 1872 expenses included in the goods station expenses.

Appendix Two

Locomotives recorded at Bath MPD
by the Revd Alan Newman

Class	Type	Locomotive Nos.

Thursday 9th August, 1934

Class	Type	Locomotive Nos.
'1P'	2-4-0	92
'2P'	4-4-0	321, 326, 374, 397, 498, 509, 513, 518, 531, 561, 631, 633, 634, 635, 698
'1P'	0-4-4T	1282, 1309, 1334, 1337, 1389
'1F'	0-6-0T	1870
'3F'	0-6-0T	7316
'3F'	0-6-0	3186, 3208
'2F'	0-6-0	3527
'4F'	0-6-0	4122, 4136, 4167, 4271, 4277, 4461, 4523
'7F'	2-8-0	13802, 13807, 13810

Nos. 561 and 374 arrived with the down 'Pines Express'.

Friday 10th August, 1934

Class	Type	Locomotive Nos.
'1P'	2-4-0	92, 157
'2P'	4-4-0	324, 325, 326, 372, 376, 494, 496, 498, 505, 508, 512, 513, 518, 523, 524, 525, 529, 531, 539, 541, 602, 629, 630, 632, 634, 635, 696, 697, 698
'1P'	0-4-4T	1309, 1334, 1337, 1364, 1381, 1389, 1404
'1F'	0-6-0T	1870
'3F'	0-6-0T	7151 (became 7311), 7316
'3F'	0-6-0	3208, 3328, 3497
'4F'	0-6-0	3858, 3968, 4270, 4271, 4430*, 4431, 4526, 4535, 4557, 4559, 4581
'7F'	2-8-0	13801, 13802, 13806, 13807

Saturday 11th August, 1934

Class	Type	Locomotive Nos.
'1P'	2-4-0	92, 157
'2P'	4-4-0	321, 322, 325, 326, 369, 396, 461, 477, 490, 494, 496, 497, 498, 503, 505, 507, 508, 513, 517, 518, 523, 524, 525, 527, 528, 529, 531, 532, 533, 539, 541, 542, 543, 629, 630, 631, 633, 634, 635, 697, 699, 700
'3P'	4-4-0	711, 770
'4P'	4-4-0	1026, 1057
'1P'	0-4-4T	1228, 1309, 1334, 1337, 1388, 1389, 1391, 1397, 1404
'1F'	0-6-0T	1870
'3F'	0-6-0T	7151 (became 7311), 7316
'3F'	0-6-0	3180, 3208, 3344, 3436, 3439, 3461, 3712
'2F'	0-6-0	3076, 3117, 3154, 3173, 3691
'4F'	0-6-0	3858, 3875, 3912, 3925, 3968, 4035, 4135, 4270, 4271, 4276, 4405, 4424, 4430,* 4431, 4435, 4533, 4535, 4557, 4558, 4559, 4561
'7F'	2-8-0	13802, 13803, 13806, 13807

Notes
* No. 4430 had a red tender from a class '5' 2-6-0.

Appendix Three

Some Interesting Operating Details

Fastest trains milepost 133 to 133¼

Speed	Direction	Type	Engine No.	Locomotive Type	Vehicles	Date
50	Up	Express	1030	4-4-0 Compound	7 coaches	9th July, 1948
64	Down	Express	?	4-6-0 'Black 5'	8 coaches	9th July, 1948
54	Up	Stopping	?	'3P' 2-6-2T	2 coaches	29th June, 1951
65	Down	Stopping	?	'3P' 2-6-2T	2 coaches; van	22nd November, 1950
41	Up	Goods	44560	'4F' 0-6-0	8 vans	15th October, 1948
30	Down	Goods	53804	'7F' 2-8-0	47 wagons	9th August, 1948

Average speeds 1948

Up express 37 mph (9 coaches)
Down express 46 mph (6 coaches)
Up stopping 38 mph (3 coaches)
Down stopping 47 mph (3 coaches) (Class '3P' 2-6-2Ts faster than Class '2P' 0-4-4Ts)
Up goods 19 mph
Down goods 23 mph

Table of speeds/loads of more unusual locomotives, milepost 133 to 133¼

Speed	Direction	Type	Engine No.	Locomotive Type	Vehicles	Date
58	Down	Stopping	29	'3P' 2-6-2T	2 coaches	26th August, 1948
41	Down	Stopping	?	'4F' 0-6-0	2 coaches	4th September, 1948
21	Down	Stopping	3604	'3F' 0-6-0	4 coaches	8th September, 1948
57	Down	Stopping	43013	'4MT' 2-6-0	2 coaches	2nd October, 1948
53	Down	Excursion	43012	'4MT' 2-6-0	8 coaches	14th May, 1951
36	Up	Excursion	?	'4F' 0-6-0	10 coaches	11th August, 1951
15	Down	Goods	?	'Jubilee' 4-6-0	46 wagons	22nd September, 1951
30	Down	Goods	?	'3F' 0-6-0T	25 wagons	19th April, 1951
32	Up	Stopping	?	'3F' 0-6-0	8 coaches	20th August, 1954
36	Up	Stopping	44559	'4F' 0-6-0	8 coaches	3rd September, 1955
47	Down	Express	?	'4F' 0-6-0	8 coaches	4th September, 1955

Ex-GWR

Speed	Direction	Type	Engine No.	Locomotive Type	Vehicles	Date
48	Down	Stopping	?	'45XX' 2-6-2T	2 coaches	8th January, 1954
41	Down	Stopping	23	Railcar		15th April, 1954
40	Up	Stopping	?	Railcar	1 coach (ex-LMS)	19th April, 1954
40	Up	Stopping	35 & 36	Railcars	1 coach	5th June, 1954
33	Down	Stopping	28	Railcar	2 bogie vans	21st August, 1954
60	Down	Stopping	?	'45XX' 2-6-2T	3 coaches	5th October, 1954
45	Up	Stopping	?	'45XX' 2-6-2T	2 coaches	7th June, 1957
45	Down	Stopping	9795	0-6-0PT	6 coaches	10th June, 1957
42	Down	Stopping	9481	0-6-0PT	2 coaches	14th June, 1957
60	Down	Stopping	?	'45XX' 2-6-2T	2 coaches	24th June, 1957
58	Down	Stopping	?	'94XX' 0-6-0PT	2 coaches	1st July, 1957

Observations at Newton Meadows

Saturday 8th August, 1959

Loco. No.	Loco. type	Time	Type	Vehicles
82041	BR class '3' 2-6-2T	9.46 am	Down stopping	6 coaches
44966	LMS class '5' 4-6-0	10.10	Down express	8 coaches
45701	LMS 'Jubilee' class 4-6-0	10.18	Up express	8 coaches
41207	LMS class '2' 2-6-2T	10.26	Up stopping	4 coaches
73155	BR class '5' 4-6-0	10.37	Up express	8 coaches
42756	LMS 'Crab' class 2-6-0	10.50	Up express	10 coaches
3804	GWR '28XX' class 2-8-0	11.24	Down pigeon	6 vans
42968	LMS class '5' 2-6-0	11.31	Up express	10 coaches
44981	LMS class '5' 4-6-0	11.33	Down express	10 coaches
42902	LMS 'Crab' class 2-6-0	12.03 pm	Down express	10 coaches
44966	LMS class '5' 4-6-0	12.12	Up express	12 coaches
73047	BR class '5' 4-6-0	12.34	Up express	12 coaches

Saturday 2nd December, 1961

D114	BR type '4' 'Peak' class	12.09 pm	Up 'Pines Express'	10 coaches
41242	LMS class '2' 2-6-2T	12.37	Down stopping	3 coaches
92138	BR '9F' class 2-10-0	2.12	Down goods	20 wagons
92138	BR '9F' class 2-10-0	2.25	Up light engine	
73050	BR class '5' 4-6-0	2.47	Up goods	4 wagons

Wednesday 2nd May, 1962

53809	S&D '7F' class 2-8-0	6.27 pm	Up goods	29 wagons
41248	LMS class '2' 2-6-2T	6.30	Down stopping	3 coaches
41248	LMS class '2' 2-6-2T	7.06	Up stopping	3 coaches, 2 vans
44559	LMS class '4F' 0-6-0	7.09	Down goods	21 wagons

Wednesday 16th May, 1962

48468	LMS class '8F' 2-8-0	6.28 pm	Up goods	22 wagons
41240	LMS class '2' 2-6-2T	6.33	Down stopping	3 coaches, 1 van
41240	LMS class '2' 2-6-2T	7.06	Up stopping	3 coaches, 2 vans

Tuesday 16th June, 1964

D1712	Brush type '4'	6.08 pm	Up stopping	2 coaches
82036	BR class '3' 2-6-2T	6.31	Down stopping	3 coaches
48734	LMS class '8F' 2-8-0	6.33	Up goods	35 wagons

Appendix Four

Logs of Runs

Bath–Mangotsfield

	16.8.50	21.9.54	3.3.55	15.3.55	16.8.56	10.8.60	18.4.63	15.6.63	27.8.63	10.4.64	20.5.64	23.10.65
Date	16.8.50	21.9.54	3.3.55	15.3.55	16.8.56	10.8.60	18.4.63	15.6.63	27.8.63	10.4.64	20.5.64	23.10.65
Locomotive	41240	41240	41240	41240	44917	41242	41304	82041	41245	82038	82038	D1028
No. of coaches	2	2	2	2	4	4	3	3	3	3	3	3
	min. sec.											
Bath Green Park	2.15	–	–	–	–	–	–	–	–	–	–	–
Weston	–	–	–	–	–	–	–	–	–	–	–	–
Bitton	9.15	10.00	10.42	9.26	9.10*	10.42	9.43	9.42	11.33	10.01	10.42	9.54
Oldland Common	2.45	2.40	2.44	2.46	1.10*	3.07	2.45	2.43	2.57	2.49	2.37	2.28
Warmley	3.15	3.12	3.18	2.52	1.35*	3.21	3.05	2.57	3.17	3.06	2.56	3.41
Mangotsfield	3.15	3.30	3.11	2.55	2.25*(a)	3.38	3.17	3.17	3.38	3.45	3.28	4.10

Mangotsfield–Bath

	16.8.50	21.9.54	3.3.55	15.3.55	16.8.56	24.8.60	18.4.63	10.4.64	20.5.64
Date	16.8.50	21.9.54	3.3.55	15.3.55	16.8.56	24.8.60	18.4.63	10.4.64	20.5.64
Locomotive	40174	ex-GWR railcars W35, W36	ex-GWR railcar W28	ex-GWR railcar W23	41242	82004	W51148 etc.	W50660 etc.	W50684 etc.
No. of coaches	2	1	0	0	4	3	3 car dmu	3 car dmu	3 car dmu
	min. sec.								
Mangotsfield	–	–	–	–	–	–	–	–	–
Warmley	2.45	3.10	2.53	3.04	3.05	3.01	3.07	2.40	2.42
Oldland Common	2.45	3.11	2.56	3.00	3.00	2.49	2.59	2.47	3.03
Bitton	1.45	2.36	3.44	2.37	2.35	2.24	2.21	2.22	2.26
Weston	8.00	–	–	–	–	–	–	–	–
Bath Green Park	–	9.40	11.40	11.25	8.25	7.54	15.55	8.36	9.10

* Passing time.   (a) Mangotsfield North Junction

Appendix Five

Workings at Bath (Green Park)
Bank Holiday Saturday, 5th August, 1950

Up Trains

Locomotive In	Out		Arrival time
44422 40698	-	9.10 am Templecombe-Bath	11.00 *am*
44535 44557	41074	Relief to 8.40 am Bournemouth-Bradford	11.20
40696 40559	44667	8.40 am Bournemouth-Bradford	11.46
44146 45440	44847	9.25 am Bournemouth-Liverpool/Manchester	11.55
40634 44945	45265	9.45 am Bournemouth-Manchester ('Pines Express')	12.39 *pm*
568 44830	44665	9.35 am Bournemouth-Leeds	1.01
		(Unrecorded interval)	
44919		4.40 pm to Bristol (St Philip's)	-
43875 40698	42922	Relief Bournemouth-Birmingham	4.32

Down Trains

42922	569 44535	Relief Nottingham-Bournemouth	11.50 *am*
45051	40698 53805	7.30 am Nottingham-Bournemouth	11.58
40163	-	11.35 am Bristol-Bath	
		(Unrecorded interval)	
44814	?	10.25 am Manchester-Bournemouth ('Pines Express')	4.06 *pm*
41240	-	3.30 pm Bristol-Bath	4.15
44762	44945 40563	10.35 am Liverpool-Bournemouth	4.20
-	40696	3.40 pm to Templecombe	4.26

Appendix Six

Bath (Green Park) Log
7th August, 1954

Up Trains

Locomotive				Time	
In	*Out*				
40634	45449	9.45 am Bournemouth-Manchester	*arr.*	12.02 *pm*	
44810		('Pines Express')	*dep.*	12.12	
-	41241	12.23 pm to Bristol	*dep.*	12.25	
44558	44826	9.55 am Bournemouth-Leeds	*arr.*	12.37	
34043			*dep.*	12.50	
40563	44815	10.05 am Bournemouth-Cleethorpes	*arr.*	12.59	
53807			*dep.*	1.09	
44146	44165	10.35 am Bournemouth-Manchester	*arr.*	1.14	
44096			*dep.*	1.22	
40601	-	12.00 noon Templecombe-Bath	*arr.*	1.49	
44102	44035	11.12 am Bournemouth-Derby	*arr.*	2.00	
34093			*dep.*	2.06	
-	41242	2.05 pm Bath-Bristol	*dep.*	2.16	
40696	44851	11.40 am Bournemouth-Sheffield	*arr.*	2.30	
34044			*dep.*	2.44	
43436	44697	Relief Bournemouth-Tunstall	*arr.*	2.57	
53804			*dep.*	3.07	
40509	73050	Relief Bournemouth-Loughborough	*arr.*	3.25	
53806			*dep.*	3.34	
40568	41241	12.55 pm Bournemouth-Bristol	*arr.*	4.21	
40569			*dep.*	4.35	
-	42769	Light engine to Bristol	*dep.*	4.49	
44560	45239	2.45 pm Bournemouth-Bristol	*arr.*	5.19	
34040			*dep.*	5.28	
-	41240	5.38 pm to Bristol	*dep.*	5.38	
53800	-	4.15 pm Templecombe-Bath	*arr.*	6.14	
-	W35/36	6.18 pm to Bristol	*dep.*	6.18	
44561	40116	3.35 pm Bournemouth-Bristol	*arr.*	7.11	
			dep.	7.20	

Down Trains

Locomotive				Time
In	Out			
44463	40698	9.18 am Birmingham-Bournemouth	arr.	12.00 nn
	34094		dep.	12.17 pm
42769	40568	7.35 am Nottingham-Bournemouth	arr.	12.19
	34110		dep.	12.39
41242	-	12.12 pm Bristol-Bath	arr.	12.48
-	40700	1.10 pm to Templecombe	dep.	1.16
44035	-	Light engine from Bristol	arr.	1.19
42900	44560	Relief Leicester-Bournemouth	arr.	2.02
	53810		dep.	2.10
73016	40563	Cleethorpes-Bournemouth	arr.	2.19
	34043		dep.	2.33
44248	40527	9.40 am Sheffield-Bournemouth	arr.	2.40
	73052		dep.	3.00
41241	-	1.45 pm Bristol-Bath	arr.	2.49
45239	40634	7.50 am Bradford-Bournemouth	arr.	3.07
	53807		dep.	3.23
41240	-	2.29 pm Bristol-York	dep.	3.14
44775	44102	10.25 am Manchester-Bournemouth	dep.	3.46
	34093	('Pines Express')	arr.	3.55
41242	-	3.25 pm Bristol-Bath	arr.	4.05
73051	44558	10.30 am Liverpool-Bournemouth	arr.	4.15
	44810		dep.	4.26
44776	44417	10.38 am Manchester-Bournemouth	arr.	4.31
	44096		dep.	4.44
-	40696	4.35 pm to Templecombe	dep.	4.53
-	40509	Light engines toTemplecombe	dep.	5.02
	43436			
W35/36	-	4.52 pm Bristol-Bath	arr.	5.36
40116	40601	6.08 pm Bristol-Bournemouth	arr.	7.02
			dep.	7.12

Appendix Seven

Locomotives working Summer Saturdays Trains Bath (Green Park) to Mangotsfield and Bristol (Temple Meads) *by R.M. Miller*

Temple Meads dep.	Green Park arr.	Green Park dep.	Temple Meads arr.	7 Jul. 1956	4 Aug. 1956	18 Aug. 1956	25 Jun. 1960	16 Jul. 1960	3 Sep. 1960	Notes
6.05 *am*	6.42 *am*	6.55 *am* to BW								
7.11	7.49									
7.40	8.20			41208	40116					
8.20	9.00	9.05 to BW		44745	44818			42981		
9.05	9.49	9.55 to BW		44422	41243		82041	82004	82004	
				44811	44854					
12.12 *pm*	12.49 *pm*			41243	41241		41242	41243	41243	
1.45	2.24			41242	41243	41241	82041	44146	82004	a
2.29	3.08			40116	41240	40116	41304	41304	41207	
3.30	4.11			41243	41241	41242	41242			
4.52	5.35			W28	W28	W28				b
6.08	6.47	7.05 to BW		41240	41207	41207				c
7.00	7.40			40116	41240	40116				d, e
				41242	41243	41241				f
8.10	8.47			41208	40116	41240				
		6.18	6.54							
		7.01	7.40	44422						
		7.23	8.01	40116	41207			41304		
		8.11	8.49	41243	41243					
				41241				41243		
		9.53	10.33	41208	40116		41208	41207	41304	
		12.23 *pm*	1.00 *pm*	41242	41243	41241	82041	44146	82004	
		2.08	2.46	41243	41241	41242	41242		41243	
	4.23	4.30	5.14	40116	41240	40116			41207	g
	5.11	5.28	5.58	44743	45238					h
		5.45	6.30	41242		41241				
		6.18	6.55	W28	W28	W28				
	6.56	7.03	7.44	41208		41207				i
	9.53	9.58	10.31							j
		10.08	10.41							

Notes:

(a) No. 44146 ran tender-first.
(b) 4.15 pm departure from Portishead.
(c) 5.15 pm departure from Portishead.
(d) 6.15 pm departure from Portishead.
(e) To Bristol (Temple Meads).
(f) To Bath (Green Park).
(g) 12.55 pm Bournemouth (West) to Portishead.
(h) 2.45 pm Bournemouth (West) to Portishead.
(i) 3.35 pm from Bournemouth (West).
(j) 7.25 pm from Bournemouth (West).

BW   Bournemouth West

Bibliography

Books

Allsop, Niall, *Images of the Kennet & Avon*, Redcliffe (1987).

Anderson, V.R. & Fox, G.K., *Midland Railway Architecture*, OPC (1985).

Arlett, M.J. & Macdermott, B., *An Outline History of Bath Green Park Station*, Somerset & Dorset Railway Trust (1983).

Barber, R., *The Dramway*, Avon Industrial Buildings Trust (1986).

Biddle, G., *Victorian Stations*, David & Charles (1973).

Bradley, D. & Milton, D., *Somerset & Dorset Locomotive History*, David & Charles (1973).

Bradshaw's *Railway Manual, Shareholders' Guide and Directory 1869*, David & Charles (reprint 1969).

Clew, K.R., *The Kennet & Avon Canal*, David & Charles (1968).

Clinker, C.R., *Closed Stations & Goods Depots*, Avon-Anglia (1978).

Cooke, R.A., *Track Layout Diagrams of the GWR & BR WR, Section 20*, Author (1974).

Hateley, R., *Industrial Locomotives of South West England*, Industrial Railway Society (1977).

Hawkins, C. & Reeve, G., *LMS Engine Sheds, Volume 4*, Wild Swan (1984).

Macdermott, B., *Modellers' & Enthusiasts' Guide to the Somerset & Dorset Line*, Patrick Stephens (1982).

Marshall, J., *Biographical Dictionary of Railway Engineers*, David & Charles (1978).

Sims, P.T., *A History of Saltford Village*, Author (1976).

Stone, B., *Bath Millennium*, Author (1973).

Williams, F.S., *Midland Railway*, David & Charles (reprint 1968).

Wray, A., *Avon Valley & Railway 1989 Year Book*, Avon Valley Publishing (1989).

Wray, A., *Memories of the Mangotsfield to Bath Branch*, Avon Valley Publishing (1988).

Newspapers and Magazines

Bath Chronicle, Bath Herald, Bath & Cheltenham Gazette, Bath Journal, British Railway Journal No. 55 pp 262-264, *LMS Journal* No. 9 pp 3-16, *Railway Magazine*.

Acknowledgements

Grateful acknowledgements for assistance is due to: R. Adams, J. Barber, R. Ford, C.A.J. Cook, C. Davis, Revd J. Fenning, N.C. Gibbons, Mrs E.J. Gover, A. Gunning, T. Gunning, F. Holmes, J. Hopkins, E. Lockwood, D. MacCarthy, R.M. Miller, Revd A. Newman, G. Padfield, W. Powell, A.E. Rossiter, C. Smith, C. Steane, F. Staddon, J. Stamp, D.R. Steggles, T. Sullivan, D. Thorne, A. Turner, B. Ware, R. Weeks, N. White and R. Williams.

Special thanks must go to Dr T.R.N. Edwards, G. Pothecary, C. Roberts and G.A.A. Tucker who checked the manuscript.

Index

Numbers shown in **bold** refer to illustrations

At Bath goods depot: *left,* guard Frank Staddon and *right,* guard Jack Lake.

Author's Collection